HOW TO ARGUE AND WIN

HOW TO ARGUE AND WIN

by

GRENVILLE KLEISER

GYAN

Published by

GYAN

Gyan Publishing House
5, Ansari Road
Daryaganj, New Delhi-110002
Phone: 011-47034999, 9811692060
E-mail: books@gyanbooks.com

Distribution Network
gyanbooks.com
India, USA, Canada, UK, Australia, France

ISBN : 978-81-212-6035-0 (PB)
First Published, 1910

2nd Impression 2021

Printed at: Gyan Press, Delhi.

How to Argue and Win
Author: Grenville Kleiser

HOW TO ARGUE AND WIN

By

GRENVILLE KLEISER

Formerly Instructor in Public Speaking at Yale Divinity School, Yale University; Author of "How to Speak in Public," "Humorous Hits and How to Hold an Audience," "How to Develop Power and Personality in Speaking," "How to Develop Self-Confidence in Speech and Manner," etc.

1912

PREFACE

NINETY-NINE men in a hundred can argue to one who can argue and win. Yet upon this faculty more than any other depends the power of the lawyer, business man, preacher, politician, salesman, and teacher. The desire to win is characteristic of all men. "Almost to win a case," "Almost to close a sale," "Almost to make a convert," or "Almost to gain a vote," brings neither satisfaction nor success.

In this book will be found definite suggestions for training the mind in accurate thinking and the power of clear and effective statement. It is the outcome of many years of experience in teaching men to "think on their feet." The aim throughout is practical, and the ultimate object a knowledge of successful argumentation.

GRENVILLE KLEISER.

New York City,
October, 1910.

CONTENTS

I

INTRODUCTORY

THOUGHT is so wonderful and incomparable a thing that it is all the more deplorable that so many men use it indifferently. They will plan the building of a house, or a summer trip, to the smallest detail, but will permit their minds to remain in an almost continuous state of disorder.

How many men ever stop seriously to analyze the workings of their minds, or carefully to consider by what means they reach certain conclusions? Thinking, like breathing, comes so naturally to them that they do not see any necessity for study. To others thought is so complex and evanescent that any attempt at classification of ideas seems an altogether hopeless undertaking. When, however, we find men so often entangled in mental absurdities, we are led to believe that some such study is essential to clear and accurate thinking.

Disputation is carried on by most men as a spontaneous act. There are no rules by which the speaker is governed. But it should be remembered that "It is by a long, careful, patient analysis of the reasoning by which others have attained results, that we learn to think more correctly ourselves."

The mind conceives, compares, abstracts, defines, judges, and seeks to express its conclusions to other minds. Its power grows through practise, and gradually it comes to realize the truth of Pascal's exclamation: "With space the universe encloses me and engulfs me like an atom, but with thought I enclose the universe!"

Faculties that fall into disuse soon fall into disease. We should profit by the warning of Darwin who acknowledged that he almost entirely lost his taste for Shakespeare, poetry, and music, because he allowed his mind to become a kind of machine for grinding general laws out of large collections of facts. He said that if he had his life to live over again, he would make it a rule to read some poetry and listen to some music not less than once a week. He believed that a loss of these was a distinct loss of happiness, and possibly an injury to one's moral character.

Every one engages more or less in argumentation. The term does not mean contentiousness, but simply the art of persuading others to think as we do upon a given subject. We daily express our ideas, opinions, and judgments upon a great variety of matters, and in so far as we advance reasons we engage in argumentation.

Logic will not change a dunce into a philosopher, but it will put a man into more complete possession of his mental powers. It will show him how to use his knowledge to the best advantage. He must, it is true, fight his way over every inch of the ground, but logic will at least prevent him from "throwing away his blows" like one beating the air. Shorn of its terminology, it can become a study possessing real pleasure.

In the following pages will be found some simple and practical directions for developing logical precision in thought and speech. The student will do well to bear in mind that there are certain classes of men who are wholly unfitted for profitable argumentation. He will not enter into free discussion with those described by Watts:

1. The exceedingly reserved man, with little capacity for speech.

2. The imperious man, fond of imposing his sentiments upon others.

3. The dogmatical man, resisting the plainest evidence of truth.

4. The egotistical man, delighting in hearing himself talk, while the rest must be silent and attentive.

5. The unstable man, who habitually wanders from the point of a controversy.

6. The peevish man, who resents contradiction, and is swift to take offense.

7. The frivolous man, who indulges in quirks, quibbles, puns, and jokes.

8. The cunning man, who constantly seeks to take you off your guard.

Ruskin says: "The greatest thing a human soul ever does in this world is to see something, and tell what it saw in a plain way. Hundreds of people can talk for one who can think, but thousands can think for one who can see. To see clearly, is poetry, prophecy, and religion—all in one." So there are many men who can argue, for one who can argue and win. They may have good reasons, but there is lack of method, of organization of material, of force and personality. The student of argumentation must train himself to know the difference between seeing things and knowing them. Sight loiters, stays on the doorstep, but insight enters the temple. It is not so much what a man knows as the quality and form of his knowledge that distinguishes him from other men.

We shall endeavor in these pages to tell the student how to get a firm basis in truth and facts. This is the only sure ground for successful argumentation. With this as a beginning, any man of sound common sense who follows the suggestions of this book may confidently hope to learn how to argue—and win.

II

TRUTH AND FACTS

SUCCESSFUL argumentation has its proper basis in truth and may be defined as any statement or belief supported by sufficient proof. Sir William Hamilton defines truth as "a harmony, an agreement, a correspondence between our thought and that which we think about." Thomson says "Truth means that which is certain, whether we think it or not," while Goethe describes it as a huge torch which we try to steal past with blinking eyes, fearing to be burnt. Newman calls it certitude, or "the perception of a truth with the perception that it is a truth."

Our first business, then, is to get our thoughts to correspond with the facts. "The truth, the whole truth, and nothing but the truth," should be our constant aim. When we are desirous of reaching a certain place, we do not usually ask about beautiful landscapes, nor easy paths, but for the right road, and the shortest route. In our thinking habits, let the invariable question be: "Is this the truth?" We must seek truth for truth's sake, for very love of it.

In this pursuit, however, we must exercise much patience and perseverance. Before a chain of evidence is complete, many scattered links may have to be found and put in their proper places. The process is sometimes tedious—often too great for mediocre minds—but there is no other way. The man who really feels the "divine patriotism" in his soul will be satisfied with nothing less than the truth itself.

Every man has some capacity for truth. The student of argumentation should be satisfied at first to solve simple problems. Apparently insurmountable difficulties may be entirely overcome by occupying the mind with a little at a time, and working gradually from the known to the unknown. South calls truth a great stronghold, "barred and fortified by God and Nature; and diligence is properly the understanding's laying siege to it; so that, as in a kind of warfare, it must be perpetually upon the watch, observing all the avenues and passes to it, and accordingly make its approaches. Sometimes it thinks it gains a point; and presently again it finds itself baffled and beaten off; yet still it renews the onset, attacks the difficulty afresh, plants this reasoning and that argument, this consequence and that distinction, like so many intellectual batteries, till at length it forces a way and passage into the obstinate enclosed truth, that so long withstood and defied all its assaults."

In our search for truth we may at first seek lines of least logical resistance. We must make our ground good as we proceed, lest we become entangled in many diverse opinions and prejudices. It is not sufficient that our proofs be above suspicion, they must be demonstrated. The test of mature judgment rests in our ability to give it immediate expression. Certitude should produce in the mind something of the sensation one feels when the feet are upon solid ground.

We should be cautious about taking sides too soon. A free and full investigation of any subject demands that the door of our mind be wide open. As Carlyle says: "The thing is not only to avoid error, but to attain immense masses of truth." To do this successfully a man, according to Drummond, "must work, think, separate, dissolve, absorb, digest; and most of these he must do for himself and within himself."

The minds of men have in all times fluctuated between truth and error. For example, they first thought the movement of the earth to be progressive and non-rotating. At a later time, men said the earth was fixt in space and simply moved from side to side. Again, that it rotated on its own axis and moved around the sun. Limited in his grasp of absolute truth by human capacity, however, the man of science continues in his conquest of the skies.

There are some things we can not know. We know, for example, that numbers can not be brought to an end, that they are infinite, but we can not say what that infinity is. We believe God is infinite, but who can adequately describe Him?

Many of our beliefs come to us as a matter of course, or of habit, rather than from careful and deliberate reflection. We are prone to accept what others say to us without question or adequate authority, and follow blindfold many customs for no better reason than that they have been long established. We receive truths second hand, and repeat them to others, but do not possess the arguments that support them. We must cultivate the habit of thinking and judging for ourselves. The truth we first have made our own, is the only truth we can give to others.

There are two sides to every question, and we should therefore be careful not to allow prejudice to take possession of our judgment. George Eliot said, in a letter to a friend, "It is possible for two people to hold different opinions on momentous subjects with equal sincerity; and an equally earnest conviction that their respective opinions are alone the truly moral ones." Men vary in their experience; consequently they vary in their opinions. But "truth is one forever, absolute, while opinion is truth filtered through the moods, the blood, the disposition," hence the sincere seeker after truth will endeavor to discover mistakes in his own reasoning as well as in that of others.

It will be seen, then, that we should be intellectually true to the truth. Prejudice, personal interests, early training, obstinacy, and passion, must not be permitted to blind our mental vision. Our aim should be the truth, even tho we have to modify or abandon altogether long-settled and oft-exprest opinions. The presence of others should not prevent us from seeing and frankly acknowledging error when it is made clear to us. If we lose our point in public argument, we must not let our sensitiveness rob us of the truth, nor in case of victory should we make it an occasion for gloating over our opponent.

A man is not to be blamed for not assenting too soon. He properly demands valid and sufficient reasons. If he is a logical thinker, he has learned to reason with caution. He knows that his opponent may be biased by personal inclinations and motives. He desires to weigh and consider every statement. The danger of prejudice, of insufficient proof, of hasty presumption, is ever present.

The student should remember that an

ocean of truth lies all about him. It is too great for one mind, and he can at most possess only a small part. The words of Sir Isaac Newton, just before he died, are not without suggestive value: "I don't know what I may seem to the world, but, as to myself, I seem to have been only like a boy playing on the seashore, and diverting myself in now and then finding a smoother pebble or a prettier shell than ordinary, while the great ocean of truth lay all undiscovered before me."

Not the least of the pleasures of intellectual investigation is what has been called "logical satisfaction," the intrinsic pleasure of following a line of thought to a conclusion. How far a man will seek to enforce upon others the results of his truth, must depend upon himself and circumstances. He may decline to argue with a man whom he knows to be unreasonable and lacking in common courtesy. He may think it not worth while to set forth his arguments to a certain class of men who hold stubbornly to an opinion, and upon being dislodged shift to another position, and by artful dodging from place to place seem never to be cornered or embarrassed. Argumentation, even as a game of skill, is hardly worth while unless conducted under conditions that give pleasure to the participants.

Newman says that a man who is certain of a fact is slow to enter into dispute, is not disposed to criticize others, nor to become angry at their positive statements; is neither impetuous nor overbearing; avoids intemperance of thought and language; and does not impute motives to others nor accuse them of sophistry. He thinks that men have not yet attained to certitude who are impatient of contradiction, and by vehemence of assertion attempt to silence others. "A man's over-earnestness in argument," he goes on to say, "may arise from zeal or charity; his impatience from loyalty to the truth; his extravagance from want of taste, from enthusiasm, or from youthful ardor; and his restless recurrence to argument, not from personal disquiet, but from a vivid appreciation of the controversial talent of an opponent, or of his own, or of the mere philosophical difficulties of the subject in dispute. These are points for the consideration of those who are concerned in registering and explaining what may be called the meteorological phenomena of the mind, and do not interfere with the broad principle which I would lay down, that to fear argument is to doubt the conclusion, and to be certain of a truth is to be careless of objection to it—nor with the practical rule, that mere assent is not certitude, and must not be confused with it."

It is nothing less than marvelous that such men as Plato and Aristotle must have begun with their alphabet, making syllables out of letters, words out of syllables, and finally using words as the vehicle of masterly thoughts. These simple first steps, like the well-known simile of great oaks and little acorns, are characteristic of every study.

The student of argumentation, be he lawyer, politician, clergyman, public speaker, or salesman, should early seek to get a good foundation of facts. In most matters of dispute, one naturally asks: "What are the facts?" and from these he makes deductions and formulates his judgments. "Facts are stubborn things" and are indispensable to the successful advocate.

The natural indolence of man prevents him from studying a subject in all its details. He will find plausible reasons for terminating his research long before reaching accurate and final conclusions. Interruption, weariness, and a host of other excuses are advanced for slipshod work.

To get at the facts of a subject, we must proceed deliberately and carefully, satisfied with little steps at first, not ignoring even the commonplace, until at last by inexhaustible patience and application we have pursued our subject to the end. To do this with intellectual repose and unwavering faith, is to insure the most gratifying results.

What is a fact? That which can be positively demonstrated, as distinguished from a mere statement or belief. It is an agreement between a thing and what is said about it. Stephen, in his "Digest of the Laws of Evidence," says:

"A matter of fact is: (1) Everything capable of being perceived by the senses; (2) every mental condition of which any person is conscious. By a matter of fact I understand anything of which we obtain a conviction from our internal consciousness, or any individual event or phenomenon which is the object of sensation. It is true that even the simplest sensations involve some judgment: when a witness reports that he saw an object of a certain shape and size, or at a certain distance, he describes something more than a mere impression on his sense of sight, and his statement implies a theory and explanation of the bare phenomenon. When, however, this judgment is of so simple a kind as to become wholly unconscious, and the interpretation of the appearances is a matter of general agreement, the object of sensation may, for our present purpose, be considered a fact. A fact, as so defined, must be limited to individual sensible objects, and not extended to general expressions or formulas, descriptive of classes of facts, or sequences of phenomena, such as that the blood circulates, the sun attracts the planets, and the like."

The student should classify his mental material in much the same way as he would papers placed in the pigeon-holes of his desk. This gives not only a sense of security, but makes such material ready for instant use. Aristotle suggests this method of classification, when he affirms that any judgment will fall into one of these ten categories:

1. *Substance*—It is a man, a horse, etc.
2. *Quantity*—It is two cubits long, three, etc.
3. *Quality*—It is white, grammatical, etc.
4. *Relation*—It is half as large, greater, etc.
5. *Action*—It cuts, burns, etc.
6. *Passion*—It is cut, is burned, etc.
7. *Place*—It is the Agora, the Lyceum, etc.
8. *Time*—It is to-day, was yesterday, etc.
9. *Posture*—It is reclining, seated, etc.
10. *Possession*—It is having shoes, armor, etc.

It should be remembered that information is not necessarily insight. After one has the facts, he must know what to do with them, and how to apply them to advantage. We must understand the inner meaning of ideas before we can claim full possession of them. When we use such expressions as "The fact is," "As a matter of fact," "In fact," etc., we should be careful to have the evidence to support this little word "fact."

Many men do not want the facts, and it is as difficult to convince them of error as to prove to a cat that it is wrong to like mice. A disposition to dodge the real issue, and a lack of frankness in facing the real facts, is a sure and certain way to lose one's influence over the minds of other men. When a man earnestly seeks the facts and gets full possession of them, he should speak positively, if at all, since most men have a sufficient supply of doubts of their own. But if he gives expression to his beliefs before they are fully substantiated in his own mind, they may be seriously impaired by a slight contradiction, a digression, or stipulation, on the part of a casual observer. Obscurity, let it be remembered, is not always in the other man's mind, but may be in our own; nor should we forget that "In the twilight even the plainest writing is rendered illegible." Where there is a firm hold upon ideas, there will be little danger of vague speculations.

The student of argumentation will accustom himself to define his terms. He will learn to call things by their right names, and therefore will have frequent recourse to his dictionary. The rules of definition by Thomson, abbreviated here for convenience, will prove helpful:

1. A definition must recount the essential attributes of the thing defined, thus: "Words are the articulate signs of thoughts."

2. A definition must not contain the name of the thing defined; this is sometimes called arguing "in a circle."

3. A definition must be adequate—neither too narrow nor too wide.

4. A definition must not be exprest in obscure or ambiguous language, as: "The divine nature is a circle whose center is

everywhere, and whose circumference is nowhere.''

5. A definition must not be negative, where it can be affirmative, as: ''Evil is that which is not good.''

After the speaker has his facts, what then? He must know how to marshal them, and how to send them forth as a living force into the minds and hearts of men. ''Next to the knowledge of the facts and its law,'' says Emerson, ''is method, which constitutes the genius and efficiency of all remarkable men. A crowd of men go up to Faneuil Hall; they are pretty well acquainted with the object of their meeting; they have all read the facts in the same newspapers. The orator possesses no information which his hearers have not; yet he teaches them to see the thing with his eyes. By the new placing, the circumstances acquire new solidity and worth. Every fact gains consequence by his naming it, and trifles become important. His expressions fix themselves in men's memories, and fly from mouth to mouth. His mind has some new principle of order. When he looks, all things fly into their places. What will he say next? Let this man speak, and this man only."

There are many persons who have an inward conviction that they are in the wrong, but will not concede it because of stubbornness, or self-conceit, or fear of humiliation. The sincere seeker after truth should be willing and even anxious to acknowledge his error, for truth need never fear to be put on trial. But when a man feels confident he is right, that he possesses the truth, he is not to yield up his honest convictions to insolence and self-assurance. It is well to remember that error is prevalent in these days, and stalks about disguised in pretentious and even presumptuous garb. It must be recognized that it may be silenced.

Sir Leslie Stephen once said that if two and two persisted in making four, one should stop putting them together. If you don't like an inference simply do not draw it. But this will not do for the honest truth-seeker. Whether his opinions and judgments be sustained or not, whether he be condemned or vindicated by others, he persists in his earnest and unwearied search for truth—truth based upon facts.

III

CLEARNESS AND CONCISENESS

IN learning to argue and win, the student will find many valuable suggestions in the rules of formal debate. It is well understood that the effect of an argument depends much upon the clearness of the terms in which it is stated. Take the question: "Resolved, That the present distribution of power between the Federal and State governments is not adapted to modern conditions and calls for readjustment in the direction of further centralization." Before this question can intelligently be discust we must define such words as "distribution," "calls," and "centralization." Here, again, the student must resort to his dictionary for needed assistance. He will be particularly careful about the small words in his proposition, since upon one of these may hang the fate of his whole argument. Many disputes are carried to interminable lengths because the persons involved do not properly understand themselves, nor have they clearly apprehended the question.

A prolific cause of misunderstanding, even in the most ordinary matters of argument, is careless and indifferent use of words. This often furnishes a loophole of escape for those who "convinced against their will," wish to be "of the same opinion still." The word "some" is said by logicians to be a source of much error and difficulty. Its indefiniteness and unknownness render it dangerous in a proposition.

Other such equivocal words are "hence," "consequently," "then," "therefore," "because," and "accordingly." Careless use of words is humorously illustrated in the following dialog:

"How did you find your patient?"

"By going to his home."

"I mean how did you find him when you got there?"

"His wife took me to his room."

"But what shape did you find him in?"

"In the shape of a man lying on his back."

"Well, is he better?"

"If he is well, he is better, of course."

"I mean is he improving?"

"Improving what?"

"Why, his health?"

"I don't know why he should improve his health."

"Is he better, then?"

"Better than what?"

"Oh, doctor, do tell me what there is about him."

"A pair of blankets."

"Pshaw! Is he dangerous?"

"No, he is perfectly peaceable."

"Doctor, do you know how to tell what ails your patient?"

"Yes; but you don't know how to ask."

We must learn to call things by their

right names, by thinking clearly and correctly of them. These names have well been termed "handles," by which the mind grasps and retains its thought about things. The firmness with which we take hold of our thoughts, therefore, will largely determine their definiteness in actual expression. William Matthews says:

"Even the profoundest thinkers and the most accurate, hair-splitting writers, who weigh and test to the bottom every term they use, are baffled in the effort so to convey their conclusions, as to defy all misapprehension or successful refutation. Beginning with definitions, they find that the definitions themselves need defining; and just at the triumphant moment when the structure of argument seems complete and logic-proof, some lynx-eyed adversary detects an inaccuracy or a contradiction in the use of some keystone term, and the whole magnificent pile, so painfully reared, tumbles into ruins."

We should study words singly, as well

as in their context; should cultivate a taste for the best and most fitting word; should not think of words as makeshifts, but as symbols of precise and accurate thought; should realize the importance of closely scrutinizing the meaning of words, as a part of sound reasoning.

The charge that intelligent men often "talk like parrots," is not without foundation. Who has not listened to certain speakers whose words were so vague, aimless, or far-fetched, that you were forced to the conclusion they did not know what they were talking about? Another class of speakers, quite as reprehensible, so wrap their thoughts up in a profusion of words, that they are hopelessly obscure and tedious.

In his "Laws of Thought," Thomson directs attention to the four functions in which language exercises its influence upon the thinking process:

1. It enables one to analyze complex impressions.

2. It preserves or records the result of the analysis for future use.

3. It abbreviates thinking by enabling one to substitute a short word for a highly complex notion, and the like.

4. It is a means of communication.

A study of the Socratic method of dispute is recommended as a means for cultivating clarified speech; for example this from Plato:

"Tell me, Charmidas, if you knew any man who could gain the prizes in the public games, and by that means render himself illustrious, and acquire glory to his country, what would you say of him if he refused to offer himself to the combat?" "I would say," answered Charmidas, "that he was a mean-spirited, effeminate fellow." "And if a man were capable of governing a republic, of increasing its power by his advices, and of raising himself by this means to a high degree of honor, would you not brand him likewise with meanness of soul if he would not present himself to be employed?" "Perhaps I might," said Charmidas; "but why do you ask me this question?" "Because you are capable," replied Socrates, "of managing the affairs of the republic, and yet you avoid doing so, tho in the quality of a citizen you are obliged to take care of the commonwealth." "And wherein have you observed this capacity in me?" "When I have seen you in conversation with the ministers of State," answered Socrates; "for if they impart any affairs to you, I see you give them good advice, and when they commit any errors you make them judicious remonstrances." "But there is a very great difference, my dear Socrates," replied Charmidas, "between discoursing in private and contending in a public manner before the people." "And yet," replied Socrates, "a skilful arithmetician can calculate as well in presence of several persons as when alone; and they who can play well upon the lute in their closets play likewise well in company." "But you know," said Charmidas, "that fear and shame, which are so natural to man, affect us more in public assemblies than in private companies." "Is it possible," said Socrates, "that you can converse so unconcernedly with men of parts and authority, and that you should not have assurance enough to speak to fools? Are you afraid to present yourself before dyers, shoemakers, masons, smiths, laborers, and brokers, for of such are composed the popular assemblies? This is the same thing as to be the most expert in a fencing-school, and to fear the thrust of an unskilful person who never handled a foil. Thus you, tho you speak boldly in the presence of the chief of men of the republic, among whom there might perhaps be found some who would despise you, dare not, nevertheless, speak in the presence of an illiterate multitude, who know nothing of the affairs of State, and who are not capable of despising you, and you fear to be laughed at by them." "Do they not usually," said Charmidas, "laugh at those who speak best?" "So likewise," said Socrates, "do the best of men of quality with whom you converse every day; and I am surprized that you have eloquence and persuasive sense sufficient to bring these to reason, and that you think not yourself capable even to approach the others. Learn to know yourself better, Charmidas, and take care not to fall into a fault that is almost general; for all men inquire curiously enough into the affairs of others, but they never enter into their own bosoms to examine themselves as they ought. Be no longer, then, thus negligent in this matter, consider yourself with more attention, and let not slip the occasions of serving the republic, and of rendering it, if possible, more flourishing than it is. This will be a blessing, whose influence will descend not only on the other citizens, but on your best friends and yourself."

In determining a question it is advisable to have some method of testing its validity and usefulness. If its solution will serve no practical purpose, or if it be known in advance that a satisfactory explanation can not be found, it is useless to undertake it. Such questions and rules as these may profitably be considered:

1. Is it knowable?

2. Is it important, or worth while?

3. Will the probable results be commensurate with the labor involved?

4. Will it make any one wiser or better?

5. Is it within one's powers?

6. Is it stated as plainly as possible? A clearly stated question is better than an hour's confused talking.

7. Because a thing has been believed through many years is not absolute proof of its truth.

8. Because a thing has been disbelieved by many persons is not absolute proof of its error.

9. Be indifferent to everything but the truth, that you may avoid bias, and give fair consideration to both sides of a subject.

10. Avoid a mere partial examination of a subject. Get all the facts possible.

11. Avoid pet doctrines, notions, and opinions that do not rest upon sufficient grounds.

12. Control the feelings. Zeal must obey the understanding.

13. Wit does not determine a matter of controversy. A jester is a very different person from a judge.

14. When the judgment is settled upon a given question it should stand firm and not flutter in suspense.

Many a splendid thought is ruined by over-amplification. A man should know precisely how much to say, as well as how to say it. That the speaker "get to the point," is the silent but none the less emphatic desire of an intelligent listener.

Volubility is one of the most destructive forces in argumentation.

It is a necessary part of clearness that a man express his thoughts in the best sequence. John Quincy Adams says in one of his lectures on rhetoric and oratory: "You shall find hundreds of persons able to produce a crowd of good ideas upon any subject, for one that can marshal them to the best advantage. Disposition is to the orator what tactics, or the discipline of armies, is to the military art. And as the balance of victory has almost been turned by the superiority of tactics and of discipline, so the great effects of eloquence are always produced by the excellency of disposition. There is no part of the science in which the consummate orator will be so decidedly marked out, as by the perfection of his disposition."

There can be no doubt that concrete arguments are not only better for clearness, but are more powerful than abstract statements, since they are more readily apprehended and make a greater impression on the mind. For example, a man may argue against smoking on the ground that three-for-a-quarter cigars a day, for a period of twenty years, amounts to $3,444.40. Even a better argument is that of the father who was admonishing his son on this same subject. He took a five-dollar bill, rolled it into the shape of a cigaret, and put a match to it. The boy asked him in astonishment what he meant by it. The father said: "That is what you are doing every day, but with this great difference: I burned only the bill, while you are injuring yourself, and inconveniencing many others around you."

In discussions of temperance, it is doubtful if purely sentimental appeals ever have an enduring effect upon intemperate men. But you can set them seriously thinking by giving them a series of stern medical facts, such as these abridged from Dr. Henry Smith Williams:

If you take alcohol habitually you:

1. Injure your stomach, liver, kidneys, heart, blood-vessels, nerves, and brain;

2. You decrease your capacity for work;

3. You lower the grade of your mind and morals;

4. You lessen your longevity;

5. You entail misery upon your descendants.

Then he asks this pertinent question: "As a mere business proposition: Is your glass of beer, your bottle of wine, your highball, or your cocktail, worth such a price?"

There is no better test of one's thought than to give it utterance. The act of speaking stimulates many new thoughts into life. Frequently a man finds himself expressing something he did not intend, and surprized at his rich discovery accepts it in the place of his first thought. Thus thought grows through use, and the more a man exercises his mind the more prolific become his ideas.

According to Mozart's own account of his method of composing, he selected from the thoughts that went through his mind those that most pleased him, hummed them until the theme shaped and enlarged itself in his mind and showed itself there as completely as a finished picture or statue. The work, then, of committing it to paper was not a difficult task.

Likewise your clear-cut speaker is so because he is a clear-cut thinker. He does not plunge into long, intricate sentences and trust to good fortune to help him out. He does not suffer himself to grope like one in a dark and impenetrable forest. His destination is so definitely fixt in his mind that not for an instant does he lose his way. Such a thinker and speaker can readily find an audience.

There should be no hesitation about repeating a word if it is necessary to the clearness of a thought. Macaulay offers a good model for study in this respect. He did not fear to use the same word many times, when he thought it desirable, and you will find nowhere in his writings an obscure use of "he," "she," "they," the "former" and the "latter," commonly found in careless writers.

John Henry Newman's description of the poet may well be applied to the speaker and the writer, and especially to the man who would argue to win:

"He writes passionately, because he feels keenly; forcibly, because he conceives vividly; he sees too clearly to be vague; he is too serious to be otiose; he can analyze his subject, and therefore he is rich; he embraces it as a whole and in its parts, and therefore he is consistent; he has a firm hold of it, and therefore he is luminous. When his imagination wells up, it overflows in ornament; when his heart is touched, it thrills along his verse. He always has the right word for the right idea, and never a word too much. If he is brief, it is because few words suffice; when he is lavish of them, still each word has its mark, and aids, not embarrasses, the vigorous march of his elocution. He expresses what all feel, but all can not say; and his sayings pass into proverbs among his people, and his phrases become household words and idioms of their daily speech, which is tesselated with the rich fragments of his language, as we see in foreign lands the marbles of Roman grandeur worked into the walls and pavements of modern palaces."

When a man says "I know what it is, but I can not express it," he acknowledges that his thought is obscure. An idea must be clearly conceived before it can be clearly exprest. To know words intimately and to be able to choose them with precision and promptitude, is essential to successful argumentation.

IV

THE USE OF WORDS

To develop a vocabulary and style suited to argumentation, carefully read and study the great controversial writers. Accustomed to think logically, they have formed certain habits of lucid expression that may be followed to great advantage. Among such books, are to be recommended Cardinal Newman's "Grammar of Assent," James B. Mozley's "On Miracles," L. A. Lambert's "Tactics of Infidels," Horace Bushnell's "Vicarious Sacrifice," and such oratorial literature as Webster's "Reply to Hayne," and the "Lincoln-Douglas Debates."

The student of argumentation must aim at perspicuity, and for this reason he should train himself to choose the right word and put it in the right place. Anything less than this will not do. Thought is the important thing; language is only the medium through which it must shine clearly. This is why the student of English is cautioned to use as much as possible short, strong, pure, Saxon words; he should speak in the language of the people, and leave word-painting to the professional orator. Content yourself with simple words.

Newman somewhere acknowledges his indebtedness to one of his preceptors for teaching him to weigh his words, to be cautious in statements, and to obviate mistakes by anticipation.

If speaking is thinking aloud, let the student be careful about the words in which he habitually thinks. He should learn to distinguish between words of almost similar meaning. Precision can best be acquired by a close study of synonyms. For example:

Argue, dispute. We *argue* in order to make clear; we *dispute* to refute an opponent. The first may comprize a simple statement or elucidation; the second always presupposes opposition to some person. In argument we reason, in dispute we contend.

Enough, sufficient. A man has *enough* if his desires are satisfied, but it may not be *sufficient* for all his needs. If a man has what is necessary, what will adequately serve the aim proposed, he is said to have *sufficient.* A miser may have what is sufficient, yet not have *enough.*

Completed, finished. When everything is done that needs to be done, a thing is said to be *complete.* When a person has done all he intended to do, he is said to have *finished* his work.

Apt, likely. The first means suitable, or fitted; the second means probable, promising, or worthy of belief. *Likely* is often confused with *liable.* "He is liable to be there," is manifestly incorrect, as the word means accountable, responsible, and more particularly answerable to law.

Seen, appear. The first has to do with

the mind, and requires reflection or comparison, while the second is said of things *external.* You can say that the sun will *appear* in the heavens, but you can not say it will be *seen* there. *Seen* has to do with our judgment, *appear* with our senses.

Veracity, truth. One is properly applied to persons, the other to things. Men speak the *truth,* and are known for their *veracity.* It is a pleonasm to say, "A man of *truth* and *veracity.*"

Continual, continuous. The former means repeatedly, the latter means uninterruptedly. There may be *continual* rains, while the roar of the street may be *continuous.* When a thing is repeated in rapid succession it is spoken of as *continual;* but only that which is protracted and held together can be *continuous.*

Transpire, happen. The first is properly used in the sense of being made public; the second means come to pass. Secrets *transpire;* accidents *happen.* Do not confuse *chance* with these words. "If you should *chance* to meet him" is incorrect. *Chance* means fortune, luck, contingency.

Disregard, neglect. The first means indifference, the second failure to act. We *disregard* warnings and advice; we neglect duties and obligations. One may be intentional, the other merely oversight.

Partially, partly. A thing done with bias is *partially done,* a thing done in part is *partly done.* There should be no difficulty in discriminating between these words, yet they are often confused.

Invent, discover. The first means to design, devise, or produce for the first time, with the mind or imagination. The second has reference rather to things which existed before, but remained *unknown.* We can *invent* a lie, but we *discover* the truth.

Artist, artizan. To the first belong painters, sculptors, musicians, actors; to the second belong carpenters, blacksmiths, workmen. One follows an art, the other a mechanical trade.

Delicious, delightful. The first refers particularly to the pleasures of taste and smell; the second to material or spiritual objects. We speak of a *delicious* dish, or a *delightful* holiday.

Much, many. These words are often confused by careless speakers. *Much* means great in *quantity; many* means a large *number.*

If, whether. We employ if in the sense of allowing, or supposing something; we say *whether* meaning which of two, or to suggest the idea of an alternative.

It is an interesting and helpful study to trace out the differences between words of almost similar meanings, and to learn to discriminate closely and accurately in their use. The following list is suggestive for comparisons and may easily be augmented:

Acquire, attain.
Agree, coincide.

Bravery, valor.
Civil, polite.
Desire, entreat.
Deadly, deathly.
Disapprove, dislike.
Follow, succeed.
Gracious, benignant.
Harangue, address.
Harshness, acrimony.
Hesitate, demur.
Ignorant, illiterate.
Impetuous, vehement.
Justify, exculpate.
Laborious, assiduous.
Lavish, profuse.
Maintain, assert.
Malice, rancor.
Mediate, intercede.
Necessary, expedient.
Obdurate, callous.
Obstreperous, turbulent.
Occult, latent.
Panegyric, encomium.
Patient, enduring.

Possible, practicable.
Plenteous, ample.
Primary, original.
Ratio, proportion.
Reconcile, conciliate.
Research, scrutiny.
Scurrilous, insolent.
Seek, explore.
Tired, harassed.
Transcend, surpass.
Urge, incite.
Velocity, celerity.
Weighty, onerous.
Wisdom, prudence.
Yielding, submissive.
Zealous, fervent.

The student of argument will find it helpful also to make lists of words that have a particular bearing upon his study. The meaning of each should be clearly understood and fixt in the memory. He may begin with groups like these:

Reason, argue, discuss, debate, dispute, wrangle, agitate, contend, controvert.

Intellect, mind, understanding, reason, thinking, principle, intuition, instinct, conception, judgment.

Inquiry, research, analysis, examination, investigation, review, scrutiny.

Thought, reflection, cogitation, consideration, study, meditation, abstraction, speculation, deliberation, contemplation.

Evidence, facts, premises, grounds, proof, testimony.

Unreasonable, illogical, false, unsound, invalid, untenable, inconclusive, fallacious, groundless, evasive, irrelevant, flimsy, loose, vague.

Probable, likely, plausible, reasonable, specious, ostensible, presumable, credible, apparent, verisimilitude.

Possible, practicable, feasible, achieveable, compatible, conceivable.

Certain, sure, well-founded, assured, infallible, certitude, ascertained, positive, definite, absolute, indisputable, conclusive.

Accurate, definite, precise, exact, just, correct, right, tangible.

Assent, agree, accede, concur, accord, yield, acquiesce, acknowledge, admit.

Dissent, contradict, protest, repudiate, deny, oppose, rebut.

Suppose, assume, conjecture, divine, surmise, suspect, presume, fancy, believe.

Explain, define, construe, interpret, illustrate, unfold, expound, exemplify.

Truthful, sincere, candid, frank, unreserved, trustworthy, scrupulous, candid, open, veracious.

Concise, terse, brief, short, laconic, compact, pithy, exact, trenchant, succinct, epigrammatic, crisp, pregnant.

One must look intensely at words, seek to know their inner meaning, and so master them that he can bend them to his will. A vocabulary depends upon the company one keeps, not only that of books but of people. The words we habitually use are a faithful index of our thoughts. To speak clearly we must think clearly, and there can be no nobility of utterance where there is not sincerity of heart.

V

THE SYLLOGISM

THE purpose of logic is to test the validity of reasoning. The syllogism is used as a formula, consisting of three propositions, two called the premises —major and minor—which together prove the third, or the conclusion. The name syllogism literally means a reckoning all together, or the joining together in thought of two propositions. This exercise is a particularly useful one for mental discipline, and may be employed in simple forms like these:

Every man has his price.
Blank is a man.
Blank has his price.

All men are fallible.
All kings are men.
All kings are fallible.

Iron is a metal.
All metals are elements.
Iron is an element.

When the syllogism is formally stated, there must be three propositions, the conclusion coming last. Every term in the syllogism occurs twice, and must be used precisely in the same sense. In other words, there must not be the slightest ambiguity or equivocation in the use of terms, lest the correctness of the conclusion be seriously impaired.

The forms of the syllogism may be exprest, for convenience sake, in letters or syllables, thus:

B is C.
A is B.
Therefore A is C.

All A is B.
All B is C.
Therefore all C is A.

All A is B.
No A is C.
Therefore no C is B.

The names of the three terms comprizing the syllogism are illustrated by Alexander Bain, thus:

Men are fallible.
Kings are *men.*
Kings are fallible.

Fallible is the *major* term.
Men is the *middle* term.
Kings is the *minor* term.

In dealing, therefore, with an uncertain or complex argument, Bain says:

1. Ascertain what is the conclusion, or the point to be proved. State this distinctly in a proposition so as to distinguish the minor term of the syllogism and the major term.

2. Find out the middle term of the argument. In a valid syllogism there must be a middle term, and only one; and it must be something that does not occur in the conclusion.

3. Find out some proposition connecting the middle term with the major term; also

some proposition connecting the middle term with the minor term.

It is not the intention to present here an exhaustive treatment of the syllogism and its numerous forms, as an abundance of such material may readily be found in standard works of logic. The following examples are offered, however, for preliminary study and analysis. The student should examine each of these carefully, and endeavor to point out any fallacious reasoning.

You are not what I am.
I am a man.
Therefore you are not a man.

The wise are good.
Some ignorant people are good.
Therefore some ignorant people are wise.

A question neither affirms nor denies.
A judgment must affirm or deny.
Therefore a judgment can not be a question.

All planets are round.
A wheel is round.
Therefore a wheel is a planet.

THE SYLLOGISM

White is a good fellow.
Linen is white.
Therefore linen is a good fellow.

John is taller than William.
William is taller than Charles.
Therefore John is taller than Charles.

Who is the most hungry eats most.
Who eats least is most hungry.
Therefore who eats least eats most.

Stone is a body.
Man is a body.
Therefore man is a stone.

Nothing is better than wisdom.
Dry bread is better than nothing.
Therefore dry bread is better than wisdom.

Whoever kills another is a murderer.
A soldier kills another.
Therefore a soldier is a murderer.

Improbable events happen daily.
What happens daily is probable.
Therefore improbable events are probable.

HOW TO ARGUE AND WIN

He who calls you a man speaks truly.
He who calls you a fool calls you a man.
Therefore he who calls you a fool speaks truly.

No cat has nine lives.
One cat has one more life than no cat.
Therefore a cat has ten lives.

Every light can be extinguished.
The intellect is a light.
Therefore the intellect can be extinguished.

All A is B or C.
This A is not B.
Therefore this A is C

No A is C.
All B is C.
Therefore no B is A.

All C is A.
Some B is C.
Therefore some B is A.

No C is A.
All B is C.
Therefore no B is A.

All C is A.
All B is C.
Therefore all B is A.

It will be seen that the syllogism simply amounts to this: When one says that all men are fallible and that A is a man, it is only necessary that the truth of these two statements be admitted in order to make one believe that A is fallible.

The student should not be over-anxious to attempt difficult and intricate problems at the beginning of this work. A certain man once dipped into the last few chapters of a new book of geometry and mensuration. Pyramids, conic sections, and the rest so confused him that he shut the book in despair. But persuaded to begin at the beginning with lines and angles, he found pleasure in his work and at length became one of the foremost geometers of his age.

What is most needed is a mastery of plain facts, or the logic of common sense.

But this common sense is disciplined by the study and application of the syllogism, by which one learns to draw correct inferences. and conclusions from stated propositions. Logic not only recognizes the truth, but tests it. As Mill says: "If there be rules to which every mind conforms in every instance in which it judges rightly, there seems little necessity for discussing whether a person is more likely to observe those rules when he knows the rules than when he is unacquainted with them."

The student is therefore urged to study logic from a standard text-book, of which there are several, and learn the simple rules of accurate reasoning. Logic will not furnish him with knowledge, but it will teach him how best to use what he has, and whether he speak in private or in public, he will learn how to state his reasons so clearly that others can not fail to understand them.

VI

FAULTS

A FAULT common to many men is that of not thinking for themselves. They accept without question the judgments of others, and repeat them as their own. Originality with them there is none. The last man's opinion is their opinion. They make not the slightest attempt to explore mental fields on their own account, but prefer the less irksome path made by others. When prest for reasons to support their statements, they can give none, but readily relinquish their old opinions for new ones. Thus they shift from place to place, without ever finding a solid and permanent foundation.

An equally serious fault is that of permitting passion and prejudice to usurp the place of reason. Some men are so completely dominated by their feelings, that they are not amenable to the most cogent arguments. They are wholly indifferent to the opinions of others. In them violence and even vindictiveness take the place of sound and mature judgment. They would rather be wrong than be opposed in their opinions.

Loudness of voice is not necessary to convincing speech, for "Gentleness best enforces the imperial mandate." A quiet but firm tone of voice often carries the greatest weight. A man who has the facts, and knows what he is talking about, does not proclaim himself from the housetop. He is content rather to let the truth vindicate itself, and if he is required to speak, he presents his reasons with a moderation and self-possession born of certitude.

"It is a great mistake," says a writer, "and a source of half the errors which exist in the world, to yield to the temptation to allow our feelings to govern our estimate of facts. Rational religious feeling is that feeling, whatever it may be, which is excited in the mind by a true estimate of the facts known to us which bear upon religion. If we do not know enough to feel warmly, let us by all means feel calmly; but it is dishonest to try to convert excited feeling into evidence of facts which would justify it."

It is particularly desirable that the student of argumentation seek to remove all prejudice from his mind. Such an examination, if impartial, will sometimes reveal the most startling conditions. Political affiliations, early environment and education, reverence for established custom, fashion, public opinion, or self-interest, may be blinding him to the truth. He will do well not to concern himself so much about the prejudices of other men as about his own.

It is of decided advantage to see all the merits of an opponent. Many of our opinions are only provisional, and may be reversed in a moment's time. The light of to-morrow may entirely change our judgments of to-day. A new angle, a fresh piece of evidence, a different mood, suddenly may alter a life-long conception. Obscurity may be due to lack of perception, and before we suspect a speaker of vagueness we might ask him to restate his views.

There is no way in which prejudice may be so soon detected as in its dislike of opposition. A man who denies a patient hearing to another, who fears contradiction, and avowedly does not wish to hear all sides of a question, tacitly acknowledges the weakness of his own position. It was Seneca who said that, altho a man might reach a just decision without hearing the other side, yet in such a case he would not himself be just.

Addison could not endure a sharp discussion, and when he found an opponent intractable he pretended to approve. A man should not busy himself all the while with finding something to contradict, but should listen attentively that he may both appreciate and affirm. He will hear many an idea so clearly and felicitously exprest that his wonder will be that he did not say it himself.

Still another fault is that of examining a question only in part, satisfied with a one-sided view of it. To investigate all the scattered material relating to one subject may not always be possible, but the fault with many men is that they possess neither the patience nor the application to examine what is close at hand. This natural indolence is forcefully emphasized by Dr. Jules Payot, in his "Education of the Will," when he says:

"The only real antagonist that can effect the persevering will must be found in a continued force. The passions are by nature transitory; the more violent they are, the shorter their duration, except in those rather rare cases where they attain a fixity and a force bordering on insanity; therefore their intermittent character does not permit us to consider them as true obstacles to continuity of effort. There is time enough between the intervals of their attacks for a great amount of work. The real obstacle lies in a fundamental ever-present state of the mind which may be called effeminacy, apathy, idleness, or laziness. To arouse one's self constantly to fresh efforts and to renew daily the struggle against this natural state of mind, is the only way in which we may dare hope for victory."

A man should be particularly cautious about entering into argument upon subjects of religion and politics. There is always danger here, not only of loss of friendship, but of actual physical violence. Here is a somewhat humorous, but nevertheless suggestive, newspaper description of a recent dispute of this kind:

"Two men of Chatham got into a religious discussion the other day, and, in fact, it is beyond doubt, that many other men the country over were wrangling on religious differences the same day. These Chatham men could not agree as to the right interpretation to be put upon certain passages in the Bible, and nobody can find fault with them for that. If the Bible had been so explicitly worded as to have left no room for dispute regarding any of its meanings, the interest of the human mind in that wonderful book would have been much less than it has been for long centuries. It is a book that each man finds explicit enough—each in his own way. It has the gift of tongues, and each reverent reader gets his own direct personal message. But for the life of him one man can not see how another reads a meaning different from his own into certain passages.

"These two Chathamites, however, carried their religious and Christian differences to extreme lengths, for in the end one of them tried to choke the other, and was fined $5 for assault. This old—pre-Victorian—mode of enforcing a religious argument with the thumb and fingers on the windpipe of one who is found to be deficient in understanding is no longer approved by the civil, nor advised by the theological authorities. After a long and thorough trial it was agreed that while force may silence, it does not convince, an opponent in debate.

"And yet, the way some men dodge, and twist, and squirm, in argument, and close their ears and their minds to your cold, clear reasoning, makes one feel that an assault on them at $5 and costs seems like a bargain."

There is an ocean of truth all about us, and he who would learn to argue and win must be many-sided. He will derive reasons alike from men, nature, and books. He will constantly be on the alert for new information and knowledge. He will remember the Bible injunction to "Try all things, hold fast that which is good." He will make it his business to know all he reasonably can upon subjects he essays to discuss. He will have ample reasons to support his claims. By throwing the portals of his mind wide open to the admission of light from all directions, he will steadily and surely acquire breadth of vision and catholicity of spirit. He will be too big to hide behind a prejudice, and too eager for truth to be indifferent to the smallest addition to his stock of knowledge.

The differences in the understandings of men is not so much in natural capacity as in acquired habits. As exercise is necessary to the training of a strong physique, so is exercise essential to the development of a strong mind. All the rules of logic, rhetoric, and oratory will avail little without actual practise.

Lack of definite thinking is a serious hindrance to mental growth. This is responsible for much of the looseness and inaccuracy heard in every-day speech. A man can not hope to argue and win while there is uncertainty in either his thought or expression. To convince others he must first convince himself. Unless there be unmistakable definiteness in his thought, word, and expression, he will not to any great degree influence others to his way of thinking.

The student of argumentation, like the student of mathematics, must do his own sums and prove them, if there is to be real mental development. A man who takes his principles and reasons on trust, without exercising his mind, is not training himself for long reaches of thought. It has been recommended that a man should show indifference to contrary opinions in order that he may examine them without prejudice, but there should be no indifference as to choosing between truth and error. The student's object is not so much to array himself on this or that side of a subject, but so to train his mind to habits of clear and logical thinking that he will be able to make a free and comprehensive survey of a subject as a whole. His unbiased attitude of mind will lead him carefully to examine every available opinion and argument before taking a definite stand.

To argue well a man must have his proposition distinctly fixt in his own mind. He should know what he is talking about and what he is talking for. Cardinal Newman's advice to the preacher is equally applicable to any man who would engage in successful argumentation. He says:

"I would go the length of recommending a preacher to place a distinct categorical proposition before him, such as he can write down in a form of words, and to guide and limit his preparation by it, and to aim in all he says to bring it out, and nothing else."

Discursiveness, frequent use of parentheses, and over-amplification are distressing to a hearer and often fatal to an argument. No one cares to hear a man "beat about the bush," but involuntarily bids him, perhaps by a mere expression of the face, to "get to the point." The admonition to "stick to your text" applies alike to preacher and speaker.

There are many men who have good ideas on various subjects, but can not concentrate on one of them long enough to drive home a conclusion. Their chief fault is that they too easily lose sight of the main question. If a man knows "what he is driving at," let him keep that one thing constantly in view until he has accomplished his purpose. This is well illustrated in the story of the lawyer who advertised for an office-clerk. Seating the applicants in a row, he began:

"A farmer had a red squirrel that got in through a hole in his barn and stole his seed-corn. He resolved to kill the squirrel. Seeing him enter the hole one day, he took a shot-gun and fired at it, but he set the barn on fire."

"Did the barn burn down?" asked one of the boys.

"Seeing the barn ablaze, the farmer seized a pail of water, and tried to put it out."

"Did he do it?" asked another boy.

"He went inside the barn, the door was shut, and soon the barn was in full flames."

"Did he burn up?"

"The hired girl rushed out with a pail of water and—"

"Was she burned up?"

"Then the old lady came out, and all was noise and confusion, and every one was trying to put out this great fire."

"Did they all burn up?"

"Now," said the lawyer, "you have shown great interest in this story, but one of you boys has not said a single word—yes, I mean you with the red head—what have you to say for yourself?"

"I want to know," said the boy, "what became of the squirrel; that's what I want to know!"

That boy was engaged.

VII

PERSONALITY

WHY is it that when some men rise to speak every one listens, and when others do so every one begins talking to his neighbor? Is it not largely a difference in personality? There can be no doubt that next to the subject-matter itself, the manner of presenting it has much to do with success. A displeasing voice, an inflated tone, an awkward gesture, a lack of tact, or a dogmatic spirit, may utterly destroy the effect of the most profound and cogent reasoning.

The speaker's voice, as the principal vehicle of expression, should be an agreeable and flexible instrument, capable of extended modulation, and responsive to a wide range of feeling. The average voice can be developed wonderfully in a few weeks, by fifteen minutes' earnest practise daily, with exercises to be found in any good manual of elocution.

A quality that makes for success in argumentation is that of genuineness. It is disclosed in the speaker's face, voice, gesture, and manner. It may be observed even in his choice of words. Let there be the slightest pretension or insincerity, and presently it will be manifest in some part of his expression. The speaker's real character proclaims the man in spite of himself. If his disposition is to be fair and straightforward to an opponent, this will soon be recognized. A position may be defended with passionate zeal and with every available weapon, without the slightest resort to an unjust advantage.

Modesty in presenting one's views will often win a stubborn adversary. For this reason it is effective sometimes to interpose one's objections as coming from other than one's self, and in the form of inquiry rather than of infallibility. Few men like the idea of conversing with an oracle, and refuse to relinquish their right to independent judgment without at least a struggle. To conciliate them is often to win.

A successful disputant is essentially serious. It is fatal to any public man to be known only as a humorist. Wit and humor have their proper places, but to indulge in levity when important and momentous questions are under discussion is to lose weight with serious-minded men. A man who makes a practise of turning sentences into jests may soon turn friends into enemies.

A broad-minded man will willingly confess his ignorance upon certain subjects, since no one can be expected to know everything. But a man should not long remain in ignorance of the things he should know. If it be a doubtful fact, or even a word the meaning of which is not entirely clear to him, let him seek the needed information at once.

There is no better opportunity than that given by daily conversation for improving the quality of a speaker's thought and speech. He can, if he choose, direct the stream of common talk toward profitable subjects. By a tactful word or suggestion, he can so raise the level of conversation that his hearers will afterward have the conscious feeling of having been in the company of a superior mind.

Conversation offers, too, an exceptional opportunity to a man to keep himself under close observation. He can observe how well he keeps his powers in hand. Should he lose control of himself, he is as likely to lose control of others. He will avoid a dictatorial spirit, a desire unduly to thrust his views upon others, to speak presumptuously, or in any way to give offense. He will learn here to view a proposition on all sides, giving a ready ear to those who have contrary opinions to offer. A spirit of generosity toward an adversary seldom goes unrewarded. It is this beneficent spirit, indeed, that often wins in argument.

When a man seeks to drive home an argument, he should look his opponent straight in the eyes. This is the most direct communication between mind and mind. A speaker who has cultivated a vivid, versatile imagination and brings it to bear upon his subject will have little difficulty in interesting the listener. There is a charm of manner that is natural to some men, but must be cultivated by others. What is called a winning personality is almost as important in presenting certain forms of argument as are the facts themselves.

The man who would argue and win must cultivate sincerity and intense earnestness. A statement exprest with feeling and sympathy will often prove more effective than an authoritative one. Too many truths, inopportunely stated, become wearisome, and we should remember that our object is not merely to argue, but to convince and win.

We have spoken of sincerity in the speaker. This means that he should be honest both with himself and with others. As he is looking for truths, and proofs, he should give just consideration to opinions and objections advanced by an opponent. A generous manner will assure at least a patient hearing.

It is well known that the very quality of a man's voice gives weight to his argument. One instinctively turns away from certain men because of peculiarity in expression. There is a disagreeable element lurking in their speech which immediately antagonizes you. Such men must, indeed, speak unusually well in order to persuade you to their way of thinking.

A man of convincing personality, especially in driving home his arguments, must have real knowledge of other men. He should think of them as fashioned like himself, with doubts and prejudices, and with varied experiences and influences to be met and satisfied. The speaker need not relinquish his convictions, but he must be able to adapt them in new ways to meet new conditions. He should remember that truth may be uttered with such sharpness as to stab rather than enlighten.

A man who would argue and win must be fearless. This is the natural outcome of sincerity and truth. He may be positive without being dogmatic. The dogmatic man insists on assent to the form of truth, while the merely positive man states the truth clearly and firmly with due allowance for difference in the judgments of other men.

A speaker's articulation and pronunciation play a part in the impression that he makes upon others. If the vowels are well rounded, and the consonants given their full significance, the speaker's style is enhanced both in tone and effectiveness.

One can not but feel that a man who is careless in his expression is equally careless in his thought. Ideas that are clearly defined in the mind, in order to be clearly imprest upon the listener must be clearly exprest by the speaker.

The very tone of voice in which a speaker presents his arguments is important. If he speaks in too high a key, for example, he is out of tune with the listener, and to be out of tune means to be out of harmony. For this important reason a speaker will keep to his conversational tones, whether he speak privately or in public. If the nature of his subject causes him to be unusually emphatic he will depend upon intensity and earnestness rather than upon increased loudness and violence.

The importance of speech culture can not be too strongly emphasized in the building of a forceful personality. Channing well says:

"A man was not made to shut up his

mind in itself; but to give it voice and to exchange it for other minds. Speech is one of our grand distinctions from the brute. Our power over others lies not so much in the amount of thought within us as in the power of bringing it out. A man of more than ordinary intellectual vigor may, for want of expression, be a cipher, without significance, in society. And not only does a man influence others, but he greatly aids his own intellect by giving distinct and forcible utterance to his thoughts. We understand ourselves better, our conceptions grow clearer, by the very effort to make them clear to another. Our social rank, too, depends a good deal on our power of utterance. The principal distinction between what are called gentlemen and the vulgar lies in this, that the latter are awkward in manners, and are especially wanting in propriety, clearness, grace, and force of utterance."

A convincing personality manifests itself in one's carriage and walk. We are favorably imprest when we see a man with chest held high and active, his chin level and head well poised, and his walk sure and firm. An upright spine seems to betoken a like spirit in the person himself. On the contrary, a man that is awkward in appearance, with stooped shoulders, flat chest, unduly prominent abdomen, and a shuffling walk leads us to associate these characteristics of weakness with his mind and life.

To develop a strong personality a man should endeavor to be at his best even when alone. He will not have for company a set of good manners, and for himself or family a set of bad manners. On the contrary, he will so conduct himself in his private capacity that, when he stands before the public, he will act and speak naturally because it is his regular habit to do so.

It is a mistake to wait for great occasions on which to be self-confident.

This attitude of mind should be cultivated as a regular daily habit. A man may double his personality by constantly maintaining a high estimate of himself, and even by assuming the outward physical appearance of self-reliance.

Debt has been known to destroy not only a man's self-confidence, but his whole personal character. Dr. Johnson ascribed a man's downfall to debt and called it not only a calamity, but an enemy to human happiness. Some of the world's greatest men have fallen by the stroke of the insidious power of debt. One step leads easily to another. The first lapse is merely lack of punctuality in meeting an obligation. The next is deception, and probably lying. Then follow rapidly carelessness, indifference, open defiance, discouragement, despair, and failure. The burden becomes so heavy that personality is lost and self-confidence forever shattered.

Let a man pay as he goes—or not go.

It should put pride and power and self-confidence in any man to be able to stand up before the world and say, "I owe no man a dollar." And if such a man, through industry and economy, have a bank account with a decent sum of money to his credit, he has that much more reason to stand erect with assurance and independence.

VIII

THE LAWYER

THE first advice given to the lawyer is to know the law, the facts, the witnesses, and himself. Temptation to speak at too great length is common in the legal profession. The advocate is led, perhaps by over-zealousness for his client's interests, to present his case in all its details. He exhausts all the precedents of the law bearing upon his particular case, and at last reluctantly yields the matter to judge and jury.

It has been well said that a lawyer who has all the evidence on his side does not speak long, and that the best argument in a case is the statement of the case itself. Senator Beveridge says:

"A case properly stated is a case nearly won. Beware of digression. It calls attention from your main idea. It is a fault, too, which is well-nigh universal. I advise every lawyer, as a practise in accurate thought, to demonstrate a theorem of geometry every morning.''

Lord Abinger, the great English advocate, made it his habit to state, in the simplest form possible, the proposition and the leading facts to support it. He says he often opened a case in five minutes that would have taken most men nearly an hour.

The tendency to occupy too much time of the court was recently characterized by a New York judge in these words: ''It is becoming altogether too common in this city to examine witnesses at undue length, and to introduce long letters and papers. This is more confusing to the jury than it is advantageous to the cause at issue. In the interest of other litigants I regard it as my duty to expedite this case in so far as may be consistent with justice.''

The knowledge of a well-equipped lawyer covers a wide range of subjects.

He knows something about everything, and if he be a specialist, everything about something. He knows life, human nature, men, business, books, for no other profession demands as does his such diversity of mind and talent.

But when a client takes a case to him, the client expects him not only to have knowledge of the law, but to be able properly to plead his case at court—and more important still, to win. No amount of legal erudition, no plausible excuse, not even eloquence itself, will satisfy a client if he lose. The one thing paramount in his mind is that the lawyer must win his case.

The lawyer is in a very different position from that of the preacher. There is ever an adversary waiting to catch him off his guard. Every word and sentence he utters is subject to scrutiny and analysis. The whole atmosphere in which he speaks is one of debate and contention. It is a matching of ideas with ideas, facts with facts, and skill with skill. The loquacious lawyer, therefore, is an enemy to himself. He gives his opponent increased opportunities to refute, ridicule, or embarrass him. His verbosity leads him to say things he did not intend to say, possibly many of them damaging or fatal to his case. In short, he is a man described by the familiar phrase: He talks too much.

How often a lawyer begins well, makes a favorable impression, seems to be winning his case, but by talking too long wearies the court and every one within hearing of his voice. All the vitality and snap are taken out of his case, a prejudice is aroused against him, and ten chances to one he argues—to lose!

The successful advocate is a man of poise. His calmness and self-confidence inspire similar qualities in his hearers. He does not bluster or browbeat a witness; he is slow to resent smartness and even insult; he is not tempted "to give back in one's own coin"; he is sparing in his use of sarcasm and denunciation; he never knowingly takes an unfair advantage. Personalities are not arguments. The real lawyer does not threaten, but persuades; does not "play to the gallery," but speaks directly to judge and jury; does not spend his time upon trifles and quibbles, but gives his best abilities to the law and facts.

When a lawyer has prepared his case, let him closely examine it to see how much is substance and how much merely words. Has he placed his feet firmly upon facts? If so, it will require a strong adversary seriously to disturb him. If not, what chance has he against an opponent who, in addition to having the facts, may also be a trained speaker? A few points clearly and concisely stated, and prest home with proper emphasis and earnestness, are likely to be more effective in winning a favorable verdict than an over-detailed and lengthy exposition.

When a successful clergyman was asked

to indicate which sermon he considered his best, he said he was unable to say, because he endeavored to make every sermon his best. Herein is a valuable hint for the lawyer—especially the young lawyer. To every case he will give the best that is in him. At the time it will absorb his mind and attention. Nothing will be left undone that should be done. Everything possible to the winning of his case will be anticipated. He will be equal to emergencies if they arise; but, in the preparation and presentation of his case, premeditation, not accident, will govern him.

Has anger ever been known to win a cause? It is so unmistakably a sign of weakness that it repels rather than convinces an intelligent listener. Does impatience win a respectful hearing from others? We believe not, judging from our own observation. It savors too much of prejudice and small-mindedness. It exacts from others what it is unwilling to give. Does haste argue well for thoroughness and favorable results? Warren in his "Attorneys and Solicitors," says:

"No one in a hurry can possibly have his wits about him; and remember that in law there is ever an opponent watching to find you off your guard. You may occasionally be in haste, but you need never be in a hurry; take care—resolve—never to be so. Remember always that others' interests are occupying your attention, and suffer by your inadvertence—by that negligence which generally occasions hurry. A man of first-rate business talents—one who always looks so calm and tranquil that it makes one's self feel cool on a hot summer's day to look at him—once told me that he had never been in a hurry but once, and that was for an entire fortnight at the commencement of his career. It nearly killed him; he spoiled everything he touched; he was always breathless and harassed and miserable. But it did him good for life; he resolved never again to be in a hurry—and never was, no, not once, that he could remember, during twenty-five years' practise! Observe, I speak of being hurried and flustered—not being in haste, for that is often inevitable; but then is always seen the superiority of different men. You may indeed almost define hurry as the condition to which an inferior man is reduced by haste. I one day observed, in a committee of the House of Commons sitting on a railway bill, the chief secretary of the company, during several hours, while great interests were in jeopardy, preserve a truly admirable coolness, tranquillity, and temper, conferring on him immense advantages. His suggestions to counsel were masterly, and exquisitely well timed; and by the close of the day he had triumphed. 'How is it that one never sees you in a hurry?' said I, as we were pacing the long corridor, on our way from the committee-room. 'Because it's so expensive,' he replied, with a significant smile. I shall never forget that conversation; and don't you."

The successful lawyer must be mentally alert. He is continually called upon to form quick judgments, and the more he trains himself in advance to "think on his feet," the better will he acquit himself in court. Webster and Lincoln early in life were members of debating clubs, and so had frequent practise in the art of extemporaneous address. Every lawyer should join a speaking club of some kind, or if there is not one in his neighborhood, he should organize one.

Assertions are not proofs. A lawyer is judged, not only by what he says, but by what he does. Let him proceed to his proofs promptly and unequivocally. If he can not win by a fair presentation of the facts, he has no right to win. A reputation for sterling integrity is one of the strongest arguments a lawyer can possess. Such a man has much in his favor even before he utters a single word. It is said of Lincoln that the simple fact of his being on a particular side of a case gave to it a distinct advantage.

A fund of good illustrations, pointed anecdotes, and facts drawn from actual experience, are valuable auxiliaries to the legal advocate. He must, however, be sure to use them opportunely. They arouse special attention and this causes the listener closely to observe their particular application to the subject under discussion. If the analogy be not good, they quickly notice it, and the illustration falls flat.

We have said that the lawyer should speak concisely, but it is equally important that he use plain and simple language. An argument may be wholly obscure to the average jury, if overloaded with technical, unfamiliar, and high-sounding words. The style known as "legal phraseology," to be found in formal documents, need not be imported to any large extent into the lawyer's speech. He should seek to reach and impress the mind of his hearer in language that is common to that hearer, be he carpenter, mechanic, teacher, or physician.

Does emotion play any part in modern legal pleading? It does. With very rare exceptions, where only the baldest facts are set forth, a man speaks with feeling. He can not help doing so if he be in earnest. Thought and emotion are almost inseparable. The degree of the speaker's belief in what he utters colors the tones of his voice surely tho often unconsciously. Without really attempting to do so, he reaches his listeners through the heart as well as through the mind.

Should he affect a dramatic style of speaking in court? Should he purposely play upon the emotions of a jury? Very seldom. Should he suggest by word or action the thought either of "elocution" or oratory"? It would be better if he did not. For the most part he should aim to be a plain, straightforward, earnest speaker, a man speaking to other men, with voice and manner appropriate to the subject and occasion. He may rise to unusual heights in the earnestness of his appeal, he may be completely carried away by his overmastering sincerity, but if he be well trained he will at no time violate the principles of natural speech.

There are cases where sympathy undoubtedly plays an important part in the advocate's appeal for clemency or acquittal. But emotion to be effective must be real. If it is overwrought, or hollow, or excessively dramatic—if, in other words, it does not ring true, it may do more harm than good. The best appeal is that which springs unexpectedly and spontaneously out of the speaker's heart. No premeditation, no pretense, no empty "working on the feelings," but a strong, deep, sincere desire for justice. The advocate should state nothing he can not prove. A writer has well said:

"Nothing is gained, but, on the contrary, a great deal is lost, by stating to the jury anything you can not prove. The jury are not convinced by your speech, but by the evidence. You can not hope to achieve more with the most impressible juryman than to bring him to this: 'Well, if you prove what you say, you will have my verdict.' In accordance with this state of feeling on the part of the jury, your course will be only to describe your testimony in the course in which it will least disturb the order of the story, as it already exists in their minds. You will take the witnesses, therefore, in order of time, and shortly repeating that portion of the narrative which is spoken to by the witness you are about to introduce, state who and what he is, and the circumstances, if any, that give peculiar value to his testimony, or that enabled him to depose to the particular facts, and then very shortly repeat the facts he will prove. If he speaks also to a subsequent part of the transaction, when you have said all you have to say of the former part, and not before, refer to that latter part with the like introduction and the like brevity."

Several volumes might be written on the fine art of cross-examination. Here all the skill, tact, and patience of the lawyer are often required. Witnesses vary widely in temperament and mental capacity. They are reluctant or defiant. But the lawyer takes them in hand, and kindly but persistently leads them along toward the facts he seeks to establish. This requires rare discretion, good temper, definiteness of aim, and adaptability.

We have emphasized the importance of the most thorough preparation in the conduct of a legal case. The advocate must be ready, however, for many emergencies, and for new and difficult problems that will be disclosed only at the trial itself. A trial has well been called "a legal battle," upon which both sides enter believing they are in the right.

Frequently a man doesn't know whether he is in the right or not. He thinks he is, but his opponent thinks otherwise. Only a contest can determine who is right. The counsel on either side receives many a surprize during a protracted trial—a new piece of evidence, an uncertain witness, a concealed letter or agreement, an unexpected discovery—whatever it may be, the skilful lawyer must know instantly how best to meet it.

How much may turn upon even a single incident is illustrated in the case of Grayson, charged with the murder of Lockwood. The principal witness, Sovine, testified that he saw Grayson run away immediately after firing the fatal shot. Interest in the trial was intense, and feeling ran high against the prisoner. When the prosecution rested, the lawyer for the defense, who had been very quiet throughout the trial, stood up and said:

"And you were with Lockwood just before and saw the shooting?"

"Yes."

"And stood very near them?"

"No; about twenty feet away."

"May it not have been ten feet?"

"No; it was twenty feet."

"In the open field?"

"No; in the timber."

"Beech timber. Leaves on it are rather thick in August?"

"Rather."

"And you think this pistol the one used?"

"It looks like it."

"You could see defendant shoot—see how the barrel hung, and all about it?"

"Yes."

"How near was this to the meeting-place? Three-quarters of a mile away?"

"Yes."

"Did you not see a candle there, with Lockwood or Grayson?"

"No! what would we want a candle for?"

"How, then, did you see the shooting?"

"By moonlight!"

"You saw this shooting at ten at night —in beech timber, three-quarters of a mile from the lights—saw the pistol barrel—saw the man fire—saw it twenty feet away—saw it all by moonlight? Saw it nearly a mile from the camp lights?"

"Yes; I told you so before."

Then the lawyer slowly took an almanac from his pocket, offered it in evidence, and read from it that on the night in question the moon was not visible but arose at one o'clock the next morning.

The witness, Sovine, who was subsequently arrested as the real murderer, broke down and confest.

The lawyer was Abraham Lincoln.

It is sometimes advisable to show your recognition of the other side's arguments, and even to concede them. Lord Abinger, in his autobiography, says:

"Very often, when the impression of the jury and sometimes of the judge has been against me on the conclusion of the defendant's case, I have had the good fortune to bring them entirely to adopt my conclusions. Whenever I observed this impression, but thought myself entitled to the verdict, I made it the rule to treat the impression as very natural and reasonable, to acknowledge that there were circumstances which presented great difficulties and doubts to invite a candid and temperate investigation of all the important topics that belonged to the case, and to express rather a hope than a confident opinion that upon a deliberate and calm investigation I should be able to satisfy the court and jury that the plaintiff was entitled to the verdict. I then avoided all appearance of confidence, and endeavored to place the reasonings on my part in the clearest and strongest view, and to weaken that of my adversary; to show that the facts for the plaintiff could lead naturally but to one conclusion, while those of the defendant might be accounted for on other hypotheses; and when I thought I had gained my point I left it to the candor and good sense of the jury to draw their own conclusion. This course seems to me not to be the result of my consummate art, but the plain and natural course which common sense would dictate. At the same time it must be observed that he who would adopt it can only expect success when it is known that he can discriminate between a sound and a hopeless case, and that his judgment is sufficiently strong to overcome the bias of the advocate and the importunity of the client, and to make him at once surrender a case that can not and ought not to be sustained."

The lawyer will still find scope for eloquence in the law court—not rhetorical claptrap and offensive bombast—but genuine man-to-man talking. He can not do better than keep in mind Dr. Johnson's definition of oratory as "the power of beating down your adversaries' arguments, and putting better in their places."

There must not be more force than is required, lest he appear like one who "wields a huge, two-handed sword to extricate a fly from a spider's web."

Concise rules for the lawyer:

1. Be dignified.
2. State the facts.
3. Don't quibble.
4. Keep your voice low.
5. Don't threaten.
6. Mean what you say.
7. Conceal your desire to win.
8. Shouting is not eloquence.
9. Never show discouragement.
10. Be ready for emergencies.
12. Concentrate on your main chance.
13. Be brief.
14. Familiarize yourself with both sides.
15. Make common sense the basis.
16. Be self-confident.
17. Keep your eye on the goal.
18. Never abuse opponents or witnesses.
19. Cultivate matter-of-fact speaking.
20. Save your strong points until the last.

IX

THE BUSINESS MAN

THE life of modern business is inspired largely by interchange of ideas and opinions. The heads of many houses meet daily in close conference to determine questions of business policy and to discuss important problems. At such meetings it is the man with ideas, one who can formulate his arguments clearly and effectively, who wins.

The average business man has occasion daily to use his powers of argumentation. Perhaps the price of goods has been advanced; forthwith the customer must be given good and sufficient reasons. Or a letter of complaint from out-of-town requires that a representative be sent immediately to satisfy the disgruntled correspondent. In numerous ways a business man must be ready to meet daily emergencies, all more or less demanding the gift of persuasion.

Misunderstanding in business, due to lack of clearness of ideas or of expression, is a prolific cause of litigation. It may be that a man does not know how to say precisely what he means, or at the moment does not really know what he means. As a result he becomes entangled in a tedious and expensive lawsuit. The records of courts show that in thousands of cases a little more clear and careful reasoning would have obviated trouble.

The value of silence in the business man is often quite as important as correct and forceful speech. A talkative man may easily say too much, and in an unguarded moment betray to watchful competitors the most vital secrets of his business. Many customers dislike much talking, and prefer to do their business quietly and in their own way. It is just here that a man must use tact and discretion. To say too little may as readily give offense as to say too much.

There are times when one of the strongest arguments that can be offered is a firm but pleasant "yes," or "no." Many men, however, lack the faculty of positive assertion. They make up their minds to say "no," but for lack of proper reasons to back up their decision, they capitulate at the first appearance of formidable argument.

To be able to argue successfully in business, a man must not only have the facts but the ability to put them together. At the head of a large commercial business in New York is a young lawyer who, through long training under the most able men of his profession, has developed a mind of rare logical acuteness. Why was he selected for this important trust? Because he is a man with a trained mind. He can take a business matter of any description, reduce it to its smallest elements, and present it in the clearest and most forceful manner to his associates. He is paid for his brains. So great is his ability that he can on short notice argue either side of a case with equal success. His logical and argumentative powers place him in immediate control of any matter under discussion, and he has not the slightest difficulty in convincing others of the correctness of his opinions. In short, he has the gift of presentation.

Next to having the facts of his business, a man should possess a full degree of earnestness by which he can enforce his points and make others believe as he does. A half-hearted manner in speech is almost surely fatal. Earnestness can best be developed through belief in one's self and the power of self-excitation. The mind is first stored with reasons that are unassailable; then the speaker charges himself with a strong feeling that he is right, that there is no other way to bring about the desired end, that it means much to him and his associates, and furthermore that he will drive home these reasons with all the power of his being, that he will compel others to his way of thinking, that he will positively win. Such thoughts repeated to himself will generate a full supply of self-excitation, and at the proper time he impresses his opinions and beliefs upon others by sheer force of personality.

The business man should cultivate agreeable manners. This insures at least a good hearing, and often a favorable one. He can be pleasant without being weak. Opposition and contrary opinions should be met patiently and generously. He may even yield minor points to win the larger aspects of his case. Such a man will sometimes win with comparatively weak arguments as against a pugnacious and disagreeable man who fails properly to use strong ones.

There is an expert connected with a certain house who lacks the power of statement. When asked his opinion on a subject, one side looks quite as good to him as the other. He can not bring himself to take a positive attitude. Another fault of his is that he never has his facts ready. He must look them up, or he will tell you to-morrow. The result is that, altho he has expert knowledge of his business, for lack of clear statement he carries no weight with other men.

Sincerity is an essential part of successful business argumentation. It is akin to earnestness and one may be said to complement the other. When a man is sincere, when he has diligently studied out his subject in all its details, when he believes in his mind and heart that he is right, he becomes a formidable opponent in almost any kind of argument. Sincerity based upon facts is not readily dislodged. If facts are stubborn things, they are particularly so when exprest by a man who is at once earnest, agreeable, positive, and sincere.

The president of one of the largest manufacturing concerns in this country, with headquarters in New York, spends almost every day of his business life in conference with the heads of different departments. Possibly a strike has taken place at one of their factories, and he calls in some of his most trusted men. They must devise means of settling the difficulty, and they proceed to discuss the question whether they will accede to the demands of the strikers or fight them. On such an occasion it is men who can present their reasons lucidly and convincingly that stand highest with the company.

Or possibly a question of competition arises. How is it to be met? Certain men are called in, who are expected to present good ideas and arguments. If they can the president is satisfied; if they can not he sends for other men. He wants the man who can argue well. The head of a business house once sent a man out of the conference because he could not present his ideas clearly. He was in the way. A befuddled brain is a hindrance on such an important occasion.

A company thinks of erecting a new building somewhere, and immediately there is a call for the best men to talk it over. The president wants to know their opinion of the location, whether it should be on a railroad convenient for easy shipments, or in the center of the town for local delivery. Maps are called for and the merits of various locations are discust. Here, again, the man of clear-cut, logical mind, who can seize instantly upon all the points of a situation and present them forcefully, wins the day. It would astonish an outsider to know in what detail such a matter is discust. How high should the building be? What space should be allotted to each department? When should it be built? A hundred vital questions must be answered.

Next the president of the company calls in the heads of the traffic department. He wants to know the rate to Texas or to some other point. The men must have the answers at their tongue's end. Rates are perhaps too high, and one of the men must go to the railroad and by force of argument induce it to lower its rates.

Again, the managers of the different factories are called in from all parts of the country and closely interrogated. Why are the shipments being delayed, and what is the cause of so many complaints? These and numerous other questions must be answered in a careful, diplomatic and convincing manner; otherwise the services of such men will be no longer required.

In every big house are hundreds of sales agents, whose duty it is to employ good salesmen and to bring them together every day for an earnest talk about ways and means. They must secure capable men and inspire them with enthusiasm for their work. Usually these sales agents have a regular meeting-room, where they talk to their salesmen about the goods and the best methods of salesmenship. They endeavor to inspire their men to greater effort.

In every business, great and small, there is constant need for argument in some form or other. To succeed in these days of keen competition, the heads of a business house must be men of large reasoning powers, with ability for clear, logical, accurate statement, and possessing the gift of forceful speech. These qualities can be cultivated through conscientious study. The various suggestions offered throughout this book apply equally to the business man. He should set his mind in order, learn the precise and accurate use of words, study the syllogism, strengthen his mental forces by wide and profound reading, and develop by daily practise his varied powers of expression. Voice, face, manner, and personality must be made his obedient servants, by which he can impress his thoughts and beliefs upon others with convincing power.

X

THE PREACHER

A CLERGYMAN recently said, "I try to sell the 'gospel,' but find few buyers." Here is a tacit acknowledgment of failure. If a man representing a business house should return from a trip and report to his firm that he had tried to sell their goods but found "few buyers," they would not long retain his services. The preacher, not unlike the salesman, must be able to present clear and convincing arguments to secure even a proper hearing; then he must follow up his advantage with sufficient force and fervor to persuade the listener to act. This is successful "salesmanship" in preaching.

It is easy to find fault with the Church, and possibly this fault-finding is too common and often misdirected. But it would startle one into serious thinking to hear a leading New York clergyman assert, as one did recently, that the modern house of worship is a cold-storage plant, that there are too many messageless sermons, and that preachers fail to teach truths of which people stand in greatest need.

What, then, shall the preacher do? First of all, he should have the truth. He should know what he is talking about, and speak as much as possible out of his own living experience. His truth must be made interesting to others. A modern congregation prefers the short road in argument. A long chain of reasoning is too difficult and taxing for them to follow; they prefer the truth in homeopathic doses, and that the preacher should not attempt to prove too much. Illustration is better than abstract statement, and graphic reference to a recent event is more impressive than philosophical disquisition. Controversy, criticism, and condemnation should be employed sparingly. "It is better," says a writer, "to hold honestly one fragment of truth in the midst of immeasurable error, than to sit alone, if that were possible, in the midst of an absolute vision, clear as the hyaline, but only repellent of falsehood, not receptive of truth."

But equally important to effective preaching is delivery. It argues in favor of a speaker that he has himself well in hand. The effect of the most cogent argument may be utterly destroyed by a weak voice, an artificial tone, or a clumsy gesture. The preacher will do well to remember that there is a well-defined prejudice against the importation of anything "theatrical" into the pulpit. The art of the actor is fundamentally different from the work of the preacher. At best the actor only represents, imitates, pretends, and acts. The actor seems to be; the preacher must be.

It is to be feared, however, that this prejudice has narrowed many preachers down to a pulpit style almost devoid of warmth and action. In their endeavor to avoid the dramatic and sensational, they have refined and subdued many of their most natural and effective means of expression. The function of preaching is not only to impart, but to persuade; and persuasion demands something more than an easy conversational style, an intellectual statement of facts, or the reading of a written message. The speaker must show in face, eye, hand, arm, the whole animated man, in fact, that he himself is moved before he can hope successfully to persuade and inspire others.

The modified movements of ordinary conversation do not fulfil all the requirements of the preacher. These are necessary and adequate for the groundwork of the sermon, but for the supreme heights of passionate appeal, for strong argumentation, when the soul of the preacher would leap from its body in the endeavor to reach men, there must be intensified life and action—dramatic action.

Poise is power, and reserve and repression are parts of the dignified office of the preacher, but carried too far may degenerate into weak and unproductive effort. Perfection of English style, rhetorical floridness, and profundity of thought will never wholly make up for lack of appropriate action in the work of persuading men.

The power of action alone is vividly illustrated in the touch of the finger to the lips to invoke silence, or the pointing to the door to command one to leave the room. The preacher might often find it profitable to stand before a mirror and deliver his sermon exclusively in pantomime in order to test its power and efficacy.

The body must be disciplined and cultivated as assiduously as the other instruments of the speaker. There is eloquence in attitude and action no less than eloquence in voice and feeling. A preacher drawing himself up to his full height, with a significant gesture of the head, or with flashing eye pointing the finger of warning at his hearers, may rouse them from indifference when all other means fail.

Sixty years ago the Rev. William Russell emphasized to his fellow preachers the importance of visible expression. He said of the preacher:

"His outward manner, in attitude and action, will be as various as his voice; he will evince the inspiration of appropriate feeling in the very posture of his frame; in uttering the language of adoration, the slow-moving, uplifted hand will bespeak the awe and solemnity which pervade his soul; in addressing his fellow men in the spirit of an ambassador of Christ, the gentle yet earnest spirit of persuasive action will be evinced in the pleading hand and aspect; he will know, also, how to pass to the stern and authoritative mien of the reprover of sin; he will, on due occasions, indicate, in his kindling look and rousing gesture, the mood of him who is empowered and commanded to summon forth all the energies of the human soul; his subdued and chastened address will carry the sympathy of his spirit into the bosom of the mourner; his moistening eye and his gentle action will manifest his tenderness for the suffering; his whole soul will, in a word, become legible in his features, in his attitude, in the expressive eloquence of his hand; his whole style will be felt to be that of heart communing with heart."

Dramatic action gives picturesqueness to the spoken word. It makes things vivid to the slow imagination, and by contrast invests the speaker's message with new meaning and vitality. It discloses, too, the speaker's sympathy and identification with his subject. His thought and feeling, communicating themselves to voice and face, to hand and arm, to walk and posture, satisfy and impress the hearer with a sense of adequacy and completeness.

Henry Ward Beecher, a conspicuous example of dramatic style in preaching, was drilled for three years, while at college, in voice-culture, gesture, and action. His daily practise in the woods, during which he exploded all the vowels from the bottom to the top of his voice, gave him not only a wonderfully responsive and flexible instrument, but a freedom of bodily movement that made him one of the most vigorous and virile of American preachers. He was in the highest sense a persuasive pulpit orator.

A sensible preacher will avoid the grotesque and the extreme of mere vivacity. Incessant gesture and action, undue emphasizing with hand and head, and all suggestion of self-sufficiency in attitude or manner should be guarded against. All the various instruments of expression should be made ready and responsive for immediate use, but are to be employed with that taste and tact that characterize the well-balanced man. Too much action and long-continued emotional effort lose force, and unless the law of action and reaction is applied to the preaching of the sermon the attention of the congregation may be lost and so the desired effect be utterly destroyed.

The face as the mirror of the emotions is an important part of expression. The lips will betray determination, grief, sympathy, affection, or other feeling on the part of the speaker. The eyes, the most direct medium of psychic power, will flash in indignation, glisten in joy, or grow dim in sorrow. The brow will be elevated in surprize, or lowered in determination and perplexity.

The effectiveness of the whisper in preaching should not be overlooked. If discreetly used it may serve to impress the hearer with the profundity and seriousness of the preacher's message, or to arrest and bring back to the point of contact the wandering minds of a congregation.

To acquire emotional power and dramatic action the preacher will study the great dramatists. He will read them aloud with appropriate voice and movement. He will study children, men, and nature. He will, perhaps, see the best actors, not to copy them, but to stimulate his taste and imagination.

The intimate relationship between the voice and the spirit of the speaker suggests that one is necessary to the fullest development of the other. The voice can interpret only what has been awakened and realized within; hence nothing discloses a speaker's grasp of a subject so accurately and readily as his attempt to give it expression in his own language. It is this spiritual power back of words, developed principally through the intuitions and emotions, that gives psychic force to speaking, and which more than logic, rhetoric, or learning itself enables the speaker to influence and persuade men.

The minister as an interpreter of the

highest spiritual truth should bring to his work a thoroughly trained emotional nature and a cultivated speaking voice. It is not sufficient that he state the truth with clearness and force; he must proclaim it with such passionate enthusiasm as powerfully to move his hearers. To express adequately the infinite shades of spiritual truth, he must have the ability to play upon his voice as upon a great cathedral organ, from "the soft lute of love" to "the loud trumpet of war."

To assume that the study of the art of speaking will necessarily produce consciousness of its principles while in the act of speaking in public, is as unwarranted as to say that a knowledge of the rules of grammar, rhetoric, or logic lead to artificiality and self-consciousness in the teacher, writer, and thinker. There is a "mechanical expertness belonging to all art," as Goethe says, and this applies to the orator no less than to the musician, the artist, the actor, and the litterateur.

Let the minister stand up even for five minutes each day, with chest and abdomen well expanded, and pronounce aloud the long vowel sounds of our language, in various shades of force and feeling, and shortly he will observe his voice developing new flexibility, resonance, and power. Let it be remembered that the voice grows through use. Let the minister cultivate, too, the habit of breathing exclusively through the nose while in repose, fully and deeply from the abdomen, and he will find himself gaining in health, tenacity, and resourcefulness.

For the larger development of the spiritual and emotional powers of the speaker, a wide and varied knowledge of men and life is necessary. The feelings are trained through close contact with human suffering, and in the work of solving vital problems. The speaker will do well to explore first his own heart and endeavor to read its secret meanings, preliminary to interpreting the hearts of other men. Personal suffering will do more to open the well-springs of the heart than the reading of many books.

Care must be taken, however, that this cultivation of the feelings be conducted along rational lines, lest it run, not to faith, but to fanaticism. There is a wide difference between emotion designed for display, or for momentary effect, and that which arises from strong inner conviction and sympathetic interest in others. Spurious and unnatural feeling will invariably fail to have an enduring effect upon men.

"Emotion wrought up with no ulterior object," says Dr. Kennard, "is both an abuse and an injury to the moral nature. When the attention is thoroughly awakened and steadily held, the hearer is like a well-tuned harp, each cord a distinct emotion, and the skilful speaker may evoke a response from one or more at his will. This lays him under a grand and serious responsibility. At such times let him keep steadily to his divine purpose, to produce healthful action, a life in harmony with God and a symphony of service."

The emotional and spiritual powers of the speaker will be developed by reading aloud each day some vigorous and passionate extract from the Bible, or Shakespeare, or from some great sermon by such men as Bushnell, Newman, Beecher, Maclaren, Brooks, or Spurgeon. The entire gamut of human feeling can be reached by thus reading aloud from the great masterpieces of literature. How shall the speaker know that he can make his own words glow and vibrate, unless he first tests and trains himself in some such manner as this? Furthermore, by thus fitting words to his mouth, and assimilating the feelings of others, he will immeasurably gain in facility and vocal responsiveness when he comes to utter his own thoughts.

Music is a powerful element in awakening emotion in the speaker and bringing to consciousness the mysterious inner voices of the soul. The minister should not only hear good music as often as possible, but he should train his ear to recognize rhythm in speech.

For the fullest development of this spiritual power in the public speaker, there should be frequent periods of stillness and silence. One must listen much in order to accumulate much. Thought and feeling must have time in which to grow. In this way the myriad sounds that arise from humanity and from nature can be caught up in the soul of the speaker and subsequently voiced by him to others.

The habit of meditating much, of brooding over thoughts, whether they be our own or those of others, will tend to disclose new and deeper meanings, and consequently deeper shades and depths of feeling. The speaker will diligently search for unwritten meanings in words; he will study, whenever possible, masterpieces of painting and sculpture; he will closely observe the natural feelings of well-bred children as shown in their conversation, and in many other ways that will suggest themselves he will daily develop his emotional and spiritual powers of expression.

The science of preaching is important, but so, too, is the art of preaching. A powerful pulpit is always one of the needs of the times. How readily does a congregation recognize a preacher of strong convictions, broad sympathies, and consecrated personality! An affectionate nature in a minister, manifesting itself in voice, face, and manner, will attract and influence men, while a harsh, rigid, vehement manner will as easily repel them.

It is feared that many sermons are written out with too much regard for "literary deportment on paper," and too little thought of their value as pulsating messages to men.

The preacher should train himself to take tight hold of his thought, to grip it with mental firmness and fervor, that he may afterward convey it to others in all its fulness and vigor. Thoughts vaguely conceived and held tremblingly in the mind will manifest a like character when uttered. Into the writing of the sermon the preacher should put vitality and intensity, and these qualities will find their natural place in delivery. Thrill of the pen should precede thrill of the voice. The habit of Dickens of acting out the characters he was depicting on paper could be copied to advantage by the preacher, and frequently during the writing of his sermon he might stand and utter his thoughts aloud to test their power and effect on an imaginary congregation.

We would emphasize the importance of the most thorough cultivation of the inner sources of the preacher, whereby the spiritual and emotional forces are so aroused and brought under control as to respond promptly and accurately to all the speaker's requirements. We would emphasize the importance of training the speaking voice as the instrument of expression and the natural outlet for thought and feeling. In the combined cultivation of these two essential parts of expression—spirit and voice—the minister will find the true secret of effective pulpit preaching.

XI

THE SALESMAN

A YOUNG man representing a publishing house, called on a photographer, and said: "Mr. X. I am not a book agent, but our firm has asked me to see you about a special art set which they feel sure you will appreciate. Their original contract calls for a thousand sets, and they have just 83 sets left. We have been selling these at $50 a set, but our contract expires in a few days, and our firm wishes to send a set of these beautiful art books to you to-morrow for only $27."

"It's a fine proposition," said the photographer, "but I am not interested in books just now."

"Better let me send you a set, they are—"

"I am very busy, and you must excuse me."

"Well," said the salesman, "I have not come to force them upon you, you know that very well. It isn't my place to try to make you take what you don't want."

This salesman certainly had not learned how to argue and win. His attitude of mind was entirely wrong, and his argument palpably weak. Failing to see that his prospective purchaser was too busily occupied properly to consider his offer, he prejudiced all his chances by hasty and ill-considered speech. His closing remark would in itself brand him as an unsuccessful salesman.

There are few men engaged in salesmanship who do not have to meet objections, and even rebuffs, in their every-day business. "If you accepted a customer's first answer as final," said a successful road salesman, "you would never secure a single order." Forewarned is forearmed, and the man who wishes to approach others on business should know precisely what to do in given circumstances. If he presents his proposition in a clear, intelligent, and concise manner, he will almost invariably receive a polite hearing. Modern salesmanship is largely a matter of common sense. This man-to-man talking style may be illustrated in the case of a traveler, say, for a glove house. It is the month of November, and the customer says:

"What are you here for, fall or spring delivery?"

"For spring delivery."

"Well, I'll tell you right now I'm not going to place a spring order."

That is very emphatic, and would ordinarily discourage an inexperienced salesman. But this traveler says quietly:

"I think you ought to."

"Why?"

"Because business will be good next spring."

"How do you know?"

"The whole tendency is that way. We have been short of goods this fall and a great many orders we have not been able to fill because the demand is greater than the supply. If you wait until next season and depend upon the market, I am very much afraid you will have some difficulty in getting your stock. This very season we are refusing half the orders that come into our place because we haven't the goods."

"But," says the customer, who is now half persuaded, "I think we are going to have dull times."

"We have had dull times," says the salesman promptly, "and now business is going to grow constantly better. It is a question of a man having the merchandise to sell. Every far-seeing man to-day says we are just in the beginning of four or five years of splendid business. You as a merchant realize that business to-day is on the ascending scale." The customer is convinced and his order is secured.

The salesman did not strain his argument at any point. He answered the questions and objections of the customer intelligently and politely. It was clear and simple common sense.

The salesman must be self-reliant, but not obtrusive. He must know the right moment to hit the nail on the head, and without fear or trembling. Said an advertising solicitor, who had been explaining the benefits to be derived from a special edition of his magazine:

"You don't need to think it over, Mr. Smith. You can decide it right now because it's right. I'll assure you it's right."

"When must you know?"

"Now!" was the laconic but firm reply—and the customer signed the contract.

Some years ago a certain New York fabric house had a printed sign that read: "In showing samples, salesmen will please refrain from making unnecessary remarks." Sometimes the best argument is silence. Many customers do not want to be told the good points about an article, but wish to judge for themselves. "We are having a great run on these goods—they are selling like hot cakes," is not the way nowadays to convince a man of intelligence. If, for example, a customer is examining a fabric, and asks, "Will this hold its color?" "Will it wear well?" or similar questions, then the salesman should be prepared to answer and to answer correctly. He should have the facts, but he should also know the right time to use them.

Another silent but effective argument in salesmanship is that of strict integrity. "Honesty is the best policy" will no longer do as a motto. It should be "Honesty is the best principle." One of the strongest arguments certain business houses have is that they maintain one price for everybody. The result is that their figures are never questioned. It is a poor argument to say "Business is business," and proceed to take advantage of a customer. The best of all arguments is service well rendered; that attracts and holds patronage.

Argument as now carried out by means of the printed word, in advertising, circularizing, and letter-writing, has become an important and interesting study. Catch phrases, with a "reason," confront the eye on almost every side. You are told that something "Chases Dirt," or "The Taste Lingers," "Wet Feet Did It," "It's a Happy Habit," or a telephone company bids you "Sit at home and let your voice travel." These are skilfully disguised arguments seeking patronage.

Hundreds of thousands of letters are mailed almost daily, for the sole purpose of securing new business. It is not too much to say that many are an absolute waste of money. They are often couched in indifferent English, and lack every semblance of convincing argument. In many instances the writers use the stereotyped phrases of others, making no attempt at originality or attractiveness. The following are familiar appeals at the close of a letter:

"Don't hesitate—act."

"Send coupon now. It costs you nothing to investigate."

"Mark the coupon now. Finding out costs nothing. Mark the coupon."

"Sign and mail the coupon at once—do it now."

"You can't afford to be without this booklet—it is free."

"This is positively the chance of a lifetime. Mail this coupon now!"

"Grasp the opportunity now—stop and mail the coupon at once."

"Writing us places you under no obligation—we are merely aiming to 'show you.'"

"Let me send my booklet to you now—it's free—and it is for you!"

These are practically in one style. The

attempt to vary them has not been successful. One appeal is no stronger than the other. Another common mistake in business letters is that of emphasizing the negative thus:

"Can you afford not to enroll with us?"

"Will you not let us hear from you with regard to enrolment in the near future?"

"You can't afford to be without this booklet."

"Send no money. Take no risk. Make no promises. Merely mail the card to-day."

"Why not write to us to-day? You can't lose anything by it. Are not the possibilities worth your while?"

This is better:

"Write to-day and learn how we can help you to a better position and bigger earnings."

This is doubtful:

"We shall watch every mail for your reply."

This is presumptuous:

"Of course you simply can not resist sending that ten dollars to-day."

This is good:

"Do it to-day and save the work of second thinking."

For the "follow-up" letter the following is disastrous:

"It is impossible to conduct a one-sided correspondence or to convince a person that something is true, when one has no intimation on what feature of the subject a doubt is entertained. If you will let me hear from you regarding the matter upon which you desire information, I shall be glad to enlighten you to the best of my ability."

The great buying public, especially the mail-order public, have grown skeptical. Glibness, self-praise, boastfulness, play upon words, and like methods of certain letter-writers attract few customers. What is most wanted are arguments supported by facts. There must be a good reason why a busy man should take the time even to sign and mail a coupon, and you can not persuade him by any such bald and peremptory request as to "do it now — this very moment — before you do another thing!"

The day is past when slipshod English is tolerated in business letters. The following atrocious example is perhaps exaggerated, but it serves as a warning:

"Our goods are the finest in the world. There ain't nothing on earth can beat 'em. We've got everybody else skinned. We don't ask nobody to take our word for it. Just look at the way we are putting them out of business! There's so-and-so, all of 'em quit in a year. We done it."

One of the largest and most successful corporations in this country issues a manual of instruction to its selling force, telling their men more particularly what they should and should not do in speech. pronunciation, argument and manner.

They hope to make theirs the model selling force in the world. Among their suggestions are to "Always acknowledge a purchase with a genuine 'Thank you, sir,' or 'Thank you, madam.' Say it out loud as if you meant it." Another is: "A salesman's good judgment ought to tell him when to talk and when to keep silent. Learn what human nature is and be governed accordingly. Look the customer straight in the eye when you address him. Show him that he is your sole concern for the time being." Scattered all through their manual are terse suggestions that are worth heeding by every man, whether he be a salesman or not, such, for example, as the following:

"There is always room behind the counter for a smiling face."

"'Thank you' can always be given in change."

"You know how you would like the salesman to act if you were his customer—that's the way."

"To get a customer's attention give him yours."

"Talk with your man, not at him, or to him."

"Good salesmen study the book of nature."

"You can have clean finger-nails without going to a manicure."

"The pleasanter you look the pleasanter you'll be."

"The man in front of you is entitled to all your attention."

"Get on the most intimate terms with the goods you sell."

"Keep thinking what the man in front of you will say when he goes out."

"Make the man who buys to-day think of coming back to-morrow."

"Good salesmanship doesn't even know failure by sight."

"Show the man with the grouch that you carry good nature in stock."

"A good countenance is the wireless telegraph of salesmanship."

The power and personality that lie in words are little understood, and seldom employed to advantage in business letter-writing. Yet what wonders can be wrought out of these twenty-six little letters of our common alphabet. Words have been well called "terrific engines," since they can either serve or destroy.

A primary requisite in a letter designed to make a strong business appeal is that it be clearly written on good stationery. Paper and envelopes should be of the best quality that particular business will warrant. Special attention should be given to paragraphing, and the general appearance of the letter should be such as to induce a careful perusal. The first object being to get the attention of the recipient, all the old stereotyped forms should be avoided. It is generally conceded that an appeal to the selfish side of the customer best wins attention, and the writer therefore makes free use of the pronoun "You."

But having attracted the reader's attention, having shown him clearly and concisely how your offering vitally concerns him, the best argument you can set forth is a straightforward recital of the merits and facts concerning what you cffer. In no other way can you hope to inspire confidence. The entire letter should breathe frankness and sincerity. You should talk directly to the reader, as if he were standing before you. Remember this is printed salesmanship. You must both convince and persuade. Whenever possible, your statements should be supported by proofs. There should be no appearance of anxiety, of desire to secure business at all hazards, of over-urging a man against his will and judgment. Books of business letter forms are of little value. What the writer must seek principally to do here is just what he would do in speech—stamp his personality upon every word, and send home thought and argument with all the force and individuality that he possesses. No one else can tell him precisely what to say. "The style is the man," here as elsewhere. He must make his own way, coin his own phrases, discover original ideas and ways of presenting them and breathe into them his own spirit. No "Ready letter writer," nothing but his own resourceful and well-trained mind, will enable him to produce a business letter that will appeal to all who read it—and win.

The close of the business letter, like the conclusion of a speech, is very important. Here the final impression is to be made, and here is determined the success or failure of the appeal. The arguments throughout have been presented in order, from weaker to stronger, but in the conclusion we come to the height of the climax, when all the powers of the writer concentrate upon one given purpose. Every word must be in its place, not a word too little or too much, and the very last word or phrase must be just the one needed to win.

The successful salesman must educate his faculties to see further than others, so that, in the face of formidable objections, he will be able to meet them with as formidable arguments, and by clearly seeing the end from the beginning maintain above everything else his clearness and self-possession.

XII

THE PUBLIC SPEAKER

A MAN constantly makes short speeches in his daily conversation. The habits formed here will largely influence and determine his public-speaking style. This offers one of the best opportunities for cultivating accuracy of statement, plain dealing, and rugged common sense. If he would argue and win upon great public occasions, he should heed these daily oportunities for small conquests.

Audiences are becoming more and more exacting. If a speaker makes a good point they see it at once, and if he doesn't make a good point they see that. They not only hear his tones and words, but closely follow the working of his mind, observe how he puts link to link in the chain of his argument, and suspend their judgment until he claims it by force of his appeal and personality.

Most public speeches are too long. There is a surplusage of words and a shortage of thoughts. "Why do you seldom preach a short sermon?" a clergyman was asked. "Because," said he, "I haven't time to prepare one." A short, pointed, worth-while speech requires more preparation and research than a long one. Almost any man can stand up and talk, but few are capable of expressing their thoughts in succinct and cohesive English. One of the best arguments for a cause is reasonable brevity. A subject may easily be ruined by too much language and over-amplification.

The public speaker should first be sure he has something worth while to say, and that he is reasonably certain of the correctness of his judgments. There is much idle, rambling, careless speech heard on every side, just as there was in Cardinal Newman's time when he said:

"'What is more common than the sight of grown men, talking on political or moral or religious subjects, in that off-hand, idle way which we signify by the word *unreal?* 'That they simply do not know what they are talking about' is the spontaneous silent remark of any man of sense who hears them. Hence such persons have no difficulty in contradicting themselves in successive sentences, without being conscious of it. Hence others, whose defect in intellectual training is more latent, have their most unfortunate crotchets, as they are called, or hobbies, which deprive them of the influence which their estimable qualities would otherwise secure. Hence others can never look straight before them, never see the point, and have no difficulties in the most difficult subjects. Others are hopelessly obstinate and prejudiced, and, after they have been driven from their opinions, return to them the next moment without even an attempt to explain why. Others are so intemperate and intractable that there is no greater calamity for a good cause than that they should get hold of it."

Whether the student intends to present his arguments in public, in business, or elsewhere, he should give special heed to the natural order in which they first arise in his mind. He should, indeed, seize this arrangement and commit it to paper. He may subsequently review it carefully and make such changes as may be deemed desirable, but the natural order mentioned is of primary importance.

There is a climactic, as well as a logical, order in thought. The proper use of this element will greatly stimulate the interest of an audience. The series should usually be in an ascending scale, with the strongest argument reserved until near the close. Spencer illustrates the danger of anti-climax in these words: "Immediately after looking at the sun we can not perceive the light of a fire.

While by looking at the fire first and the sun afterward we can perceive both; so, after receiving a brilliant, or weighty, or terrible thought, we can not appreciate a less brilliant, less weighty, or less terrible one, while, by reversing the order, we can appreciate each."

Extempore speaking is recommended as the best style for enforcing one's thought with power and effectiveness. It is more real than a speech that is read, and it is in favor with audiences. It allows the speaker to observe the effect of his ideas and arguments upon his hearers, and to alter, amplify, or repeat as he thinks best. This style enables a speaker to deliver himself with greater spontaneity and energy than would be possible if a manuscript intervened between him and his hearers. He has here the advantage of eye-to-eye communication with his audience, and can strengthen that which appears to him weak, and drive home with the most direct and positive force an idea that may be dangling in the air. The speaker should possess himself of a large fund of common sense, which Bautain urges in these words:

"Good sense is the instinctive action of right reason, discriminating with a rapidity of feeling, and by a sort of taste, what is or is not suitable in any given situation. Therefore, it is a sudden appreciation of a thousand bearings depending on circumstances, as when, amidst the fervor of delivery and from the general effect of the address—things not to be estimated by the plan alone, but declaring themselves on the instant—an idea on which stress should be laid—what part of it should be neglected—what should be comprest—what should be enlarged upon—must all be promptly seized. Then a new thought which suggests itself and must be introduced—an explanation which might run to too great a length and which must be abridged—an emotion or effect to be excited as you pass on without losing sight of the main effect—a digression into which you may enter without breaking the guiding thread of this labyrinth and while at need recovering it—all have to be judged of, decided upon, and executed at the very moment itself, and during the unsuspended progress of the discourse."

The mind of the public speaker should not only be enriched and developed by wide reading, but he should train it to hold ideas clearly and logically. He must know how to state a question correctly and boldly, and to present his ideas in their proper sequence. A study of logic will teach him how to become a clear thinker. Study and practise in public speaking will train him to "think on his feet."

Every subject has two sides. The business of the public speaker is to know both. This enables him to look at the subject in a larger view, to anticipate the arguments of an adversary, and to detect any weakness in his own. He will not then so readily be taken unawares, since "forewarned is forearmed."

Many a man feels a sense of personal insecurity in expressing his thought, for the simple reason that he has not been thorough enough in his investigation. It will not do to take for granted what other people say; we must put everything through our own mental processes in order that we may come to conclusions that will bear the test of contradiction. In his thought gathering, therefore, a man should always look for clearness and accuracy, demanding proof before he yields his judgment to another.

Next to reading the great thoughts of the world's masterpieces of prose and poetry, nothing is more valuable for the public speaker than the habit of committing choice extracts to memory and reciting them aloud at convenient moments. If this can be done in the open air, while walking in the woods, or Demosthenes-like on the seashore, in communion with nature, the results will be all the more rapid and substantial. It is surprizing how these little extracts committed to memory will sometimes come to the speaker's aid at a critical moment, as well as serve to embellish some part of an extempore speech. The night before an important session of Parliament, John Bright would read Milton for an hour or two, that he might catch something of his majesty of style.

Few speakers know how to conclude either their argument or their speech. Their thoughts fly in the air like so many fluttering ribbons, and for their life they do not know how to gather them together into a Gordian knot. Every student of this subject is advised to fix upon his destination in advance, just as one would do in making a journey. Then he will not be so likely to lose his way, and what is quite as important, to misdirect others.

Loud emphasis and fiery declamation

are not arguments. Men want the facts, and they want to consider them largely in their own way.

The greatest gift a speaker can possess is not so much that of eloquence as the power of statement. Some men are naturally lucid. Without apparent effort, they make their meaning clear at once. There is no hesitation, no apology, no ambiguity, but simple, compact common sense. These men habitually think and reason clearly, and can not help doing so in their speech.

If a man without the necessary knowledge undertakes to address an audience, he merely proclaims his own folly. It will not do to make a pretense of having the facts, for an audience quickly estimates a man at his true worth. The speaker's first object, therefore, should be to acquire a minute and thorough knowledge of his subject. As every question has two sides, he should give particular attention to any points in doubt.

He should next concern himself with the two questions: How best to recommend himself to others; and how to influence an audience to his way of thinking.

Personal character has always been regarded as an important factor in the making of an orator. If he be known as a reliable and substantial man, with sound ideas, and of sterling uprightness of conduct, this will act to his great advantage. A spirit of fair-mindedness, and a reputation for promoting the public welfare, will ingratiate a speaker in the hearts of the people.

But integrity and eloquence are not in themselves sufficient to win a great cause. The speaker must be capable of close and severe reasoning, and of skilfully putting link to link in a long chain of argument. He must conduct the hearer in the direction of his natural bent, but if he is to impress him with a sense of completeness, he must carry him beyond that. We yield ourselves readily to a man of superior knowledge, and it is only in this way that a speaker can hope to move the multitude.

The author of a little book on public speaking, published many years ago, makes an interesting distinction between eloquence and oratory. "Eloquence," he says, "belongs merely to words, oratory to the passion which fires them. The eloquence of intellect is that of speech, and sense, and symbol; but the oratory which so seldom greets the ears of men is the eloquence of the man. The philosopher only reaches the scholar, the orator reaches the mob. The philosopher talks the rhetoric of the schools, the orator the language of nature; he speaks heart words —that language which is wide as the world, which reaches humanity, which all nations understand, which the deaf and dumb can feel—the language of gratitude, of gesture—that which moves as on canvas, breathes on marble . . . . It is when the multitude are of one opinion that the orator's power is revealed; that is the seal that nature stamps upon his genius."

The student of argumentative speech should write much. Nothing is more conducive to clear and accurate reasoning than the habit of committing one's thoughts to paper. This puts them into concrete form, where they can be leisurely examined. If a link be missing it can be supplied, or if it be weak it can be strengthened. All the great orators of the world have been prodigious writers. To this habit they ascribed much of their skill as clear and precise thinkers. Thought is reined in by the use of the pen, since the hand can not move as rapidly as the mind. And just as thought becomes steady, so it becomes more stable and sure.

This habit of writing also gives a speaker style and amplitude, enabling him to express his thoughts clearly, attractively, and with due effectiveness. Should the student wish to know how simple the style of a great orator can be, let him examine the oration of Demosthenes "On the Crown," the greatest oration of all time. Cicero says that an orator should have "the acuteness of the logicians, the wisdom of the philosophers, the language almost of poetry, the memory of lawyers, the voice of tragedians, and almost the gesture of the best actors." He names three requisites for finding the lines of an argument: genius, method, and diligence. But of the three, diligence is the most important, since it is by means of that we thoroughly prepare a subject. In the one word diligence may be included the other virtues of attention, care, consideration, vigilance, assiduity, and industry.

What is the distinguishing mark of a superior mind? It is not originality necessarily, but method, by which thoughts are arranged in regular order, and distinctness of mental vision precedes clearness of expression. A mind that is governed by method knows how to classify its material, how to carry a long chain of intricate reasoning, and how to see its way clear through to the end of an argument. Emerson speaks of this power of method as constituting "the genius and efficacy of all remarkable men."

Public speaking is really a form of debate, in which the audience tho silent is none the less critical and combative. Every idea, statement, and argument of the speaker is condemned or approved almost upon the instant, and it is only when the truth is presented clearly and effectively that an audience can be won over to a favorable verdict. The speaker can not too strongly be urged, therefore, to train his mind to methodical thinking, to keep his mental data classified, and habitually to organize his thoughts in the most formidable order.

The mind must be disciplined to do its work spontaneously. The student must content himself with taking a single thought at a time, mastering it, and proceeding patiently to the next, knowing that these definite and deliberate steps are necessary for ultimate excellence. If he takes only a small part at a time, he can ultimately grasp the most difficult and complex problems.

Effectiveness in delivery involves many considerations. A speaker should have a keen sense of proportion. Just as there is a limit to a man's lifting power, so is an audience limited in its power of attention and receptivity. A long introduction or conclusion may easily rob the main part of a speech of its significance. A prime requisite for effective speaking, therefore, is to get promptly to one's subject and as promptly to conclude it. The speaker should address himself to what he knows, and ever bear in mind that it is often one single proof, properly enforced, that determines success or failure. He should say only what is necessary and willingly condense his remarks, or omit them entirely, if the occasion demands this course. Great praise has been accorded to the intellectual character of the Duke of Wellington, who displayed in his speeches the same splendid qualities of simplicity and directness so manifest in his military life. "He strips his subject," says a commentator, "of all extraneous and unnecessary adjuncts, and exposes it in its natural proportions. He scents a fallacy afar off, and hunts it down at once without mercy. He has certain constitutional principles which are to him real standards. He measures propositions or opinions by these standards, and as they come up or fall short, so they are accepted or disposed of." If men would confine themselves to what they really know, there would be less speechmaking. A speaker should at the outset find a common ground on which he and his hearers may meet. He must take them as he finds them, "speak down" to them, that there may be a point of contact. Then he may lead them skilfully along, step by step, by means of apt phrase, argument, simile, illustration, bearing them to his way of thinking.

A valuable principle of effective public speaking is that of action and reaction. At first the speaker leads the audience up to a certain pitch, and then relaxes. The next time he carries them a little higher, and again relaxes. This process, which rests the minds of the audience from time to time, is repeated as often as necessary, when suddenly the speaker hurls all his power into one strong climactic appeal, sweeps the audience off its feet—and the cause is won.

XIII

BRIEF-DRAWING

A KNOWLEDGE of brief-drawing is of great practical value to the man who would argue with force and effectiveness. It enables him to grasp his subject as a whole, to fasten it securely in his mind, and to present it in clear and logical order to others. A brief is divided into three parts, as follows:

The Introduction, which should clearly state the issue, explain the proposition, or define the terms of the discussion that is to follow.

The Discussion, which sets forth the arguments and proofs to be offered. This constitutes the main portion of a speech. The order should be climactic, leading from the known and conceded to the unknown and disputed.

The Conclusion, which sums up, or reviews, the essential points already enumerated in the discussion.

Before attempting to draw a brief, these rules should be carefully fixt in the mind.

Rule I. Set down each statement by itself.

Rule II. Make each statement clear and concise.

Rule III. Place your principal ideas as main headings.

Rule IV. Place your subordinate ideas as sub-headings.

Rule V. Indicate each and every statement by a separate symbol.

The brief is not the speech. It is a skeleton, plan, framework, or outline, which enables one to arrange his material in clear, logical, and effective order, before actually writing the speech itself. In this way much useless labor is obviated.

The procedure is not unlike that of an architect and his drawings. He carefully plans every part of his building, and by means of specifications orders just the material required for his purposes. What would be said of a man who should proceed to erect a building without any clearly defined plans? Yet the majority of men prepare a speech in precisely this way. They take a few sheets of paper, rest the head against one hand, and then commit to writing the ideas that ramble through their mind, without any special regard to order or system. The result is that the speech is usually a confused mass of material, lacking in force, clearness and cohesion. Such a speech, when delivered, is equally obscure and confusing to the listener, so that failure is not an uncommon result of such efforts.

The habit of brief-making teaches a man to be thorough and deliberate in the preparation of his speeches. It trains him to systematize his mental material: to arrange it in the most advantageous order, and to exclude everything irrelevant and immaterial. Brief-making is particularly valuable to the business man who has important letters to frame and dictate. It is valuable to every man who aims to marshal his arguments in writing, conversation, or in public speaking, as to convince others—and win.

Hereunder are given two specimen briefs, showing the affirmative side of one subject and the negative side of another. These will be of suggestive value to the student, and should enable him to make further briefs of his own.

AFFIRMATIVE BRIEF FOR A SPEECH

Subject:

THE SUFFRAGE SHOULD BE EXTENDED TO WOMAN

INTRODUCTION

A. The suffrage should be extended to woman, because

(1) She is the subject of political rights.

(2) Her capacities and claims are equal to those of men.

(3) The franchise is an element of good citizenship.

STATEMENT OF FACTS

A. The suffrage would make woman a power for good politics, since

(1) She would have a direct interest in local and national questions.

(2) She would help to make better laws.

(3) Her sphere and influence would broaden.

B. The suffrage granted to woman would better safeguard the home, since

(1) She knows best the needs of the home.

(2) She has the most vital interest in the children.

(3) She has the greatest interest in moral education.

C. It is not a valid argument against woman-suffrage to say that

(1) Some women are indifferent to it, or

(2) They would not exercise it if they could, for

(3) The same may be said of many men.

D. It is not a valid argument to say a woman is well represented by her husband, for

(1) Representation by others can not be an adequate substitute for personal responsibility.

(2) There are many unmarried women with property rights.

(3) Taxation and representation should go together.

(4) Women prefer to safeguard their own interests.

E. It can not be maintained that women are deficient in public spirit, as shown by their

(1) Widespread philanthropic work.

(2) Books and writings.

(3) Ability to discuss the questions of the day.

CONCLUSION

A. The suffrage should be extended to woman, because

(1) It is her natural right.

(2) It is part of her citizenship.

(3) It would increase her power for the general good.

(4) It would enlarge her influence.

(5) It would better safeguard the home.

(6) It would give her just representation.

B. The suffrage granted to woman would be a guarantee of

(1) Better laws.

(2) More efficient education.

(3) Elevated political and social morality.

(4) An ideal community.

NEGATIVE BRIEF FOR A SPEECH

Subject:

CAPITAL PUNISHMENT SHOULD NOT BE ABOLISHED

INTRODUCTION

A. Capital punishment has been sanctioned by custom from the earliest times, and

(1) This is a presumption in its favor.

(2) It is not brutalizing in the eyes of the public, since

(3) Many men approve it.

STATEMENT OF FACTS

A. Capital punishment acts as a deterrent to murder, as

(1) Most men fear such punishment, and

(2) Would prefer imprisonment for life.

B. If guilty men escape, it is not a valid argument against the law, because
   (1) This is due to improper enforcement, and
   (2) Is a reason for a more rigid application of the law.

C. Capital punishment is sanctioned by the Bible, as
   (1) "Who sheddeth man's blood, by man shall his blood be shed." (Genesis 9:6.)
   (2) Other Bible passages.

D. It safeguards the community in numerous ways, as from
   (1) Private revenge and
   (2) Anarchy.

E. Capital punishment should be extended,
   (1) To reach every man guilty of murder, and
   (2) To make him fear the law as inevitable.

CONCLUSION

A. Capital punishment should not be abolished, because
   (1) It is expedient.
   (2) It is just.
   (3) It relieves society of a pest.
   (4) It is in keeping with tradition.
   (5) It upholds the sanctity of human life.

B. Punishment should be neither reformatory nor vindictive, but preventive, for
   (1) Great crimes demand severe punishment, since
   (2) You can not reform a criminal by leniency, and
   (3) Our prisons are not reformatory.

XIV

THE DISCIPLINE OF DEBATE

THE art of debate is one of the best means of developing mental alertness, self-confidence, and the ability to think on one's feet. In its highest form it combines the power of the logician, the strategy of the general, the skill of the rhetorician, and the voice and grace of the orator.

The word debate literally means to strike down; hence Hamilton in his "Parliamentary Logic," says: "If your case is too bad, call in aid the party; if the party is bad, call in aid the cause; if neither is good, wound your opponent." We do not approve the latter advice, as the real object of debate should be, not personalities but principles. There will of necessity be conflict, but only of ideas and with the purpose of finding the truth. This conflict, this clash and contrast of opinion, should bring out the best that is in a man. Judgment, decision, and boldness are required in preeminent degree. Debate is not mere exhibition, but a measuring of abilities between men honestly holding opposite views upon a given subject. It requires patient drill and discipline as in military tactics, which Napoleon called the art of being the stronger. He maintained that to insure victory an overwhelming force must be concentrated upon a given point. We quote from Chambers's "Encyclopedia":

"First, as to the art of being the stronger, which is undoubtedly the highest recommendation in a general, we may cite the example of the battle of Rivoli. In 1796, Napoleon was besieging Mantua with a small force, while a very much smaller army operated as an army of observation. The Austrian commander had collected at Trent a force powerful enough to crush completely the French army, with which he was marching south. Parallel with his course lay the Lake of Garda, and to prevent the enemy escaping up one side, as he marched down the other, the Austrian leader divided his army into two powerful corps, and marched one down each side of the lake. The instant the young French general knew of this division, he abandoned the siege of Mantua, collected every available man, and marched against one body of the enemy. Tho far inferior on the whole, he was thus superior at the point of attack, and the victory of Rivoli decided virtually the whole campaign. This corresponded in principle with Napoleon's general plan in battle. He formed his attack into column, tried to break through the center of the enemy's line; and if he succeeded, then doubled back to one side, so as to concentrate the whole of his own force against one half of the enemy's, which was usually routed before the other half of the line could come up to the rescue."

A good debater, like a skilful general, thinks out everything possible beforehand. Weapons, plans, and proofs are chosen with care and precision, sometimes for weeks or months in advance. A notable instance of readiness was that of Webster in his great debate with Hayne. Much of the material used by him on that occasion had been prepared long before and reposed in his desk. Asked, after making the speech, how much time he had given to preparation, he replied, "all my life." Webster, speaking of Hayne again, said: "If he had tried to make a speech to fit my prepared notes, he could not have done it better. No man is ever inspired; I never was."

To be a successful debater, a man must keep two principal elements ever before him: convincingness and persuasion. His work does not end with merely convincing his hearers of the truth of his contentions; he must, like the genuine orator, move men to action. This, after all, is the true test of debating, as it is of, oratory.

No matter how earnest a man may be in his beliefs he should not assume infallibility. There is always the possibility of being in error, and if such be proved he should be quick to acknowledge it. A man who persists that he is right, when it has been made clear to every one present that he is wrong, simply holds himself up to possible ridicule. To resent contradiction is to be without one of the most essential qualities of a level-headed debater. The speaker should seek to explain rather than to defend. He will not protest too much. He will concede everything possible to the other side. He will despise petty advantages, and concentrate his powers on the main ideas. He will remember not to make too much of his opponent's arguments, since to elaborate them excessively would invest them with undue significance. Neither will he wholly ignore them, lest it be thought that he can not answer them. He will adopt rather a middle course, saying neither too little nor too much.

A common fault to be avoided in debate is that of protractedness. Some men insist upon having the last word. This endless reply to the reply becomes irksome to an audience. When two sides of a subject have been fairly stated, both should be willing to rest their case on that. If side issues and personalities were avoided, debates upon important questions might easily be concluded in reasonable time. The student should not forget that "The victory in a debate lies not in lowering an opponent, but in raising the subject in public estimation. Controversial wisdom lies not in destroying an opponent, but in destroying his error; not in making him ridiculous so much as in making the audience wise."

Personal invective should not be permitted to deface dignified debate. When feeling and animosity take the reins from judgment it is difficult to foretell to what extremes a speaker may not go. We do not wish to think of men debating like common scolds. Temper must not usurp the place of truth. An incident may here be noted pertaining to the speech of Charles Sumner, on "The Crime Against Kansas," delivered in the United States Senate, May 9, 1856. Mr. Douglas, Senator from Illinois, by way of resenting attacks that had been made upon him, had said:

"Sir, God grant that when I denounce an act of infamy I shall do it with feeling, and do it under the sudden impulses of feeling, instead of sitting up at night writing out my denunciation of a man whom I hate, copying it, having it printed, punctuating the proof-sheets, and repeating it before the glass, in order to give refinement to insult, which is only pardonable when it is the outburst of a just indignation."

Then followed this sharp passage at arms:

"Mr. Sumner.—The Senator has gone on to infuse into his speech the venom which has been sweltering for months—ay, for years; and he has alleged facts that are entirely without foundation, in order to heap upon me some personal obloquy. I will not go into the details which have flowed out so naturally from his tongue. I only brand them to his face as false. I say, also, to that Senator, and I wish him to bear it in mind, that no person with the upright form of man can be allowed—(hesitation).

Mr. Douglas.—Say it.

Mr. Sumner.—I will say it—no person with the upright form of man can be allowed, without violation to all decency, to switch out from his tongue the perpetual stench of offensive personality. Sir, that is not a proper weapon of debate, at least, on this floor. The noisome, squat, and nameless animal, to which I now refer, is not a proper model for an American Senator. Will the Senator from Illinois take notice?

Mr. Douglas.—I will; and therefore will not imitate you, sir.

Mr. Sumner.—I did not hear the Senator.

Mr. Douglas.—I said if that be the case I would certainly never imitate you in that capacity, recognizing the force of the illustration.

Mr. Sumner.—Mr. President, again the Senator has switched his tongue, and again he fills the Senate with its offensive odor . . . .

Mr. Douglas.—I am not going to pursue this subject further. I will only say that a man who has been branded by me in the Senate, and convicted by the Senate of falsehood, can not use language requiring a reply, and therefore I have nothing more to say."

The laws of controversy were succinctly exprest by a writer some years ago, in five simple headings that may easily be remembered:

1. Consult the improvement of those opposed to you, and to this end argue not for resentment, or gratification, or pride, or vanity, but for their enlightenment.

2. When surmising motives do not surmise the worst, but adopt the best construction the case admits.

3. To distinguish between the personalities which impugn the judgment and those that criminate character, and not to advance accusations affecting the judgment of an adversary without distinct and indisputable proof; and never to assail character (where it must be done) on suspicion, probability, belief or likelihood.

4. Never make an incriminating imputation unless some public good is to come out of it. It is not enough that a charge is true; it must be useful before it can be justifiably made.

5. Be so sure of your case as to be able to defy the judgment of mankind, and when assailed, maintain self-respect in reply, not forgetting justice to those to whom you are opposed.

The life of debate, as of any form of public speaking, is vigorous thinking. Nothing so clearly appraises a man's knowledge at its true value as spirited public argument. It discovers a man to himself. Repeated experience will prove to him that he can not be too well prepared for such a contest. Several ways are open to him in the delivery of his speech:

1. He may write out his speech in full and read it to his audience. This is the least effective of all.

2. He may write it out and memorize it, but in this case the memory is likely to speak instead of the personality.

3. He may write it out and memorize the more important parts. Here the audience will be likely to observe the

difference between that which is memorized and that which is extempore.

4. He may speak from notes or headings. This method has some advantages, but usually leads to unevenness in delivery.

5. He may wholly extemporize. This is the ideal form of delivery. It does not imply lack of preparation. On the contrary, it exacts the most careful premeditation on the part of the speaker. Nothing must be left to chance. This does not mean, however, that the speaker is to depend upon his recollective forces, to try simply to recall what he has written out on paper, but at the moment of speaking his creative powers are to be fully liberated and he is to speak out of the fulness of his knowledge and his experience.

XV

TACT

It is generally conceded that Mark Antony won his hearing before the Roman mob by his incomparable tact. His speech is worthy of careful analysis by any one desirous of knowing how to argue and win. Observe the tact there is in these few lines:

I come not, friends, to steal away your hearts:
I am no orator, as Brutus is;
But, as you know me all, a plain blunt man,
That loved my friend; and that they know full
well
That gave me public leave to speak of him.
For I have neither wit, nor words, nor worth,
Action, nor utterance, nor the power of speech,
To stir men's blood: I only speak right on;
I tell you that which you yourselves know,
Show you sweet Cæsar's wounds, poor dumb
mouthed,

And bid them speak for me: but were I Brutus,
And Brutus Antony, there were an Antony
Would ruffle up your spirits, and put a tongue
In every wound of Cæsar, that should move
The stones of Rome to rise and mutiny.

There are many objectionable phrases used by careless speakers. No one can hope to secure the good-will of an opponent by saying: "I disagree with you," "That's just where you're wrong," "You are dreadfully mistaken," "That is absurd," "You're on the wrong track," "Don't tell me that," "You don't know what you're talking about," "That is ridiculous," or "I don't believe it." A tactful man will be more likely to say, "Have you carefully considered so and so?" "I believe some one has said," "There is good authority for the statement," "Many persons think," "You will, perhaps, agree," "Does it not impress you that?" "Should we not give weight to?" "Have you heard the argument of?" "How do you account for?" "I may appear stupid, but would you mind making that a little more clear to me?" These and like expressions have an easy conciliatory effect, especially upon a stubborn opponent, and where, for other reasons, it is impossible wholly to win an argument, the speaker leaves at least a favorable impression. Let the student of argument learn as soon as possible that many things which he thinks of are not necessarily things to be said. A thought or word must be withheld at will. He must be quick to recognize unexpected situations, and to adapt himself promptly to new conditions. He will make his points without resorting to unkindness or unfairness. He will not seek to belittle his opponent. He will remember that he is dealing with facts—not with personalities. Positive thought, clearly stated, is what he most needs. If there be any scolding, it will be left to his opponent to indulge in.

There is tactful silence. "Be swift to

hear,'' says an old writer, ''but be cautious of your tongue, lest you betray your ignorance, and perhaps offend.'' Many men do not know when to stop, nor how long to stop. Silence is a powerful aid to persuasive argument. It shows the other man that you are a willing listener, and impresses him with your fair-mindedness. It gives you time to formulate your own reasons, and to compare with them the arguments of others. The habit of judicious silence also saves a man from much idle talking. It has been said of Cardinal Newman that when he spoke he always had something worth while to say, that he said it as no one else could say it, and that, even in ordinary conversation, his supreme loyalty to truth was invariably evident.

In Proverbs we read: ''He that answereth a matter before he heareth it, it is folly and shame unto him.'' And again: ''Happy is the man that findeth wisdom, and the man that getteth understanding.

For the gaining of it is better than the gaining of silver, and the profit thereof than fine gold. She is more precious than rubies; and none of the things thou canst desire are to be compared unto her. Length of days is in her right hand; in her left hand are riches and honor. Her ways are ways of pleasantness, and all her paths are peace. She is a tree of life to them that lay hold upon her; and happy is every one that retaineth her."

The tactful man takes a middle course, avoiding obstinate dogmatism on the one side, and a too ready acquiescence on the other. He avoids even the suspicion of being arbitrary or unyielding. He concedes a little and often gains much. He knows that if he grants nothing to the other side, nothing will be granted to him. He expresses himself not too positively, lest he drive his hearer away.

Tact manifests itself in the little things of every-day life. Some persons seem to have been born upside down. They see everything in unnatural and reversed order. They have an unfortunate way of always presenting the ugly side of things, and of saying the disagreeable word. Some are so misguided as to think it well to have a reputation for being brutally frank. "You will excuse my candor," they bravely plead, "but I say just what I think."

Tact may be observed in the little everyday affairs of people. "Pardon me, madam," said a woman to another, as she stept up behind her, "but your dress is unfastened at the back." "Well," said she, turning around suddenly, "suppose it is, it's none of your business, is it?" Contrast with this the case of a tactful woman who alighted from a street-car accidentally on another's dress, ripping it at the waist. The offended person frowned ill-naturedly, but the first woman said pleasantly, "Will you please let me help you to pin that?" and the frown was lost in a smiling assent.

Lack of tact is really lack of common sense. It is not tactful to tell long-winded, tiresome, hackneyed stories, nor to speak of the disagreeable and offensive. To joke at the other man's expense may raise a laugh at the time, but may lead to serious after consequences.

The tact of a public speaker should show him how long to speak, when to abridge his remarks, and when in certain circumstances entirely to omit speaking. Who has not been bored to death by the tactless man who rises to speak at a late hour, intent upon giving his speech just as he prepared it, and unwilling to forego even a single paragraph?

A tactful speaker will not begin by telling at great length of things he does not intend to prove, and does not intend to say. He will not announce his subject as being divided into twenty-three or more parts, and each part subdivided into as many others. Proper tact will prompt him to proceed to his subject without unnecessary delay, and to present his ideas and arguments clearly and forcefully.

It is not tactful to plunge heedlessly into a conversation not knowing where one is going to come out. Too many people talk without the slightest consideration for the rights of others. This is particularly noticeable in public places where a single loud voice may make quiet conversation impossible. Tact is taste. Tact knows what to do and how to do it. Tact would rather say nothing than give offense. Tact counsels in time and gives a phrase its proper direction even after it is half-uttered. Tact is always graceful and in face of sudden danger makes haste to conciliate.

When Sidney Smith overtook a man in the street whom he mistook for a friend, and slapped him on the back, the man gave him a look which caused him to say, "I beg your pardon, I thought I knew you—but I'm glad I don't!" It is the Irishman who can make perfect use of tact.

When asked by two ladies which he thought the older, he answered, "To tell you the truth, you each look younger than the other." "How did you like our Easter music?" a church-member recently asked a visitor. "I thought," was the tactful reply, "that all the members of the choir did their very best."

XVI

CAUSE AND EFFECT

FINAL cause is never known, since no matter how far back we wished to go the mind would seek to inquire further. The very elusiveness of the search is a source of never-ending pleasure to the truth-seeker. The idea of cause and effect arises in the mind as naturally as any other law. We see a certain thing invariably lead to a certain result, we call one the cause and the other the effect. The idea is pertinently put by Dr. Martineau when he asks: "If it takes mind to construe the world, how can it require the negation of mind to constitute it?"

The study of cause and effect clearly shows the existence of immutable laws in the ordering of the world. It would be difficult to think of the world as otherwise. Henry Drummond speaks somewhere of a child's book called "The Chance World," where everything happened by chance. The sun might rise, or it might not; a person who jumped up in the air might not come down again. With cause and effect gone, and law annihilated, such a world would be a lunatic asylum with lunatics as inmates. Causation may be considered under three heads:

1. Practical causation, as applied to everyday occurrences as we see them. For example, one man shoots another, and we say the man killed the other. This is sufficient to serve our ordinary purposes in stating the cause.

2. Scientific causation, which takes into consideration all the antecedent circumstances. For example, to describe the cause of a flower would embrace many considerations besides the germ itself, such as air, sun, light and heat.

3. Causation of force or energy, or

the "Conservation of Energy," by which force and what becomes of it are fully explained.

The student of argumentation should cultivate an inquiring mind that will carry him back of symbols, properties and conditions, to the things or causes themselves. This habit of closely analyzing a subject was conspicuous in Lincoln, whose mind, it is said, "ran back behind facts, principles and all things, to their origin and first cause—to that point where forces act at once as effect and cause. He would stop in the street and analyze a machine. He would whittle a thing to a point. He was remorseless in his analysis of facts and principles."

In this study of cause and effect it is easy to fall into error. For example, Mill says: "When a man is shot through the heart, it is by induction that we know it was the gun-shot which killed him, for he was in the fulness of life immediately before, all circumstances being the same, except the wound." Whereupon Jevons says Mill overlooks the "multiplicity of circumstances, and that a cause is usually, if not always, the conjunction of many circumstances." Then he proceeds to ask whether, because one man pricks his finger and dies, all men who prick their fingers die? or because one man goes to sea and suffers from nausea, all men who go to sea must necessarily suffer from nausea?

A blow on a man's head, if the blow be severe enough, will cause death, but a blow on the head does not always cause death. Whether the obscurity that arises from a plurality of causes is a defect of our own minds need not be entered upon here, but what has been said will be sufficient to start the student thinking on his own account and to exercise discretion in forming his conclusions.

Many years ago Watts wrote his excellent treatise on "The Improvement of the Mind." His valuable suggestions for studying cause and effect are quoted here for the student's benefit:

"When we are inquiring into the causes of any particular effect or appearance, either in the world of nature, or in the civil or moral concerns of men, we may follow this method:

"1. Consider what effects or appearances you have known of a kindred nature, and what have been the certain and real causes of them. For like effects have generally like causes, especially when they are found in the same sort of subjects.

"2. Consider what are the several possible causes which may produce such an effect, and find out, by some circumstances, how many of those possible causes are excluded in this particular cause. Thence proceed by degrees to the probable causes till a more close attention and inspection shall exclude some of them also, and lead you gradually to the real and certain cause.

"3. Consider what things preceded such an event or appearances, which might have any influence upon it; and tho we can not certainly determine the cause of anything merely from its going before the effect, yet among the many forerunners we may probably light upon the true cause, by further and more particular inquiry.

"4. Consider whether one cause be sufficient to produce the effect, or whether it does not require a concurrence of several causes; and then endeavor, as far as possible, to adjust the degrees of influence that each cause might have in producing the effect, and the proper agency and influence of each."

When we are inquiring into the effects of any particular cause or causes, we may follow this method:

"1. Consider diligently the nature of every cause apart, and observe what effect every part or property of it will tend to produce.

"2. Consider the causes united together in their several natures and ways of operation; inquire how far the powers or properties of one will hinder or promote the effects of the other, and wisely balance the proportions of the influence.

"3. Consider what the subject is, upon which the cause is to operate; for the same cause on different subjects will often produce different effects, as the sun, which softens wax, will harden clay.

"4. Be frequent and diligent in making all proper experiments, in setting such causes at work, whose effects you desire to know, and putting together, in an orderly manner, such things as are most likely to produce some useful effects, according to the best survey you can take of all the concurring causes and circumstances.

"5. Observe carefully all the events which happen either by an occasional concurrence of various causes, or by the industrious application of knowing men; and when you see any happy effect certainly produced and often repeated, treasure it up, together with its known causes, among your improvements.

"6. To take a survey of all the circumstances which attend the operation of any cause, or causes, whereby any special effect is produced, and find out, as far as possible, how far any of those circumstances have a tendency either to obstruct, or promote, or change those operations, and consequently how far the effect might be influenced by them."

XVII

READING HABITS

It is natural for man to pursue knowledge, and to wish to develop his God-given capacities to the highest degree. It is equally natural for him to wish to impart his knowledge to others. Men, however, are often sluggish in mind and body, and their powers must be roused into action through some special influence. Once this mental and physical indolence is overcome, they derive genuine pleasure from study and reading.

To be an exact thinker, a man must be an exact reader and observer. This may be acquired through self-discipline. He can read books without becoming bookish. He has constant opportunities of reasoning for himself about what he reads, hears and sees on all sides.

One of the most important and valuable sources of knowledge is the reading of good books. The reader's object is not merely to understand words, or "to contradict and confute," or "to believe and take for granted," but to get clear-cut ideas and make them his own. The multiplicity of books in these days renders it difficult to choose wisely. A man may well inquire: Is this book worth while? Do I read it because a friend, who perchance may not know my needs, recommends it? What purpose will it serve? Will it contribute anything to my mental growth, my happiness, my general development? What, really, is the object of my reading — amusement, information, knowledge, or spiritual uplift? What should guide me in my choice of books? To sift the worth-while books from the annual output of thousands of volumes requires taste and judgment. A man may stock his library shelf full with books, and leave his mind unfurnished.

Schopenhauer describes the difference between the self-thinker and the book philosopher as revealed in their manner of delivery. That of the first is earnest, direct, original; the other dull, flat and conventional. To read for a definite purpose gives mental alertness, since the reader is anxious to absorb all he possibly can. One may put this to the test by trying to recall anything he has ever read in an aimless desultory fashion. A man should read to confirm and supplement his own ideas. He should feel that he is constantly building himself. He will, therefore, reflect upon what he reads. He will read both sides of a question in order to determine for himself where the weight of truth rests. His object should never be merely to be able to talk copiously and with the appearance of many-sided knowledge. He is not to aim at being a plausible talker, but a convincing and persuasive speaker. Reading is a means to an end, and we must never substitute literature for life, nor reading for thinking.

In his inspiring book on "The Practise of Self-Culture," Hugh Black says: "The best education grows from the broadening intelligence that comes through eye and ear and the simple experiences of life. The man who forms the habit of observation in its widest sense lives in a world that grows wider and richer, and finds in it an inexhaustible source not only of increasing knowledge, but also of fresh wonder and delight. The profoundest wisdom is always that which is being constantly verified by contact with nature and with life." This explains the peculiar delight to be found in reading a good book in God's out-of-doors. In the woods, at the seashore, or on the great ocean, a book takes on a new charm and helpful influences seem to be all about the reader.

One should read to secure clear and settled notions of things, in order that he may be able correctly to judge the statements of other men and correctly set forth his own. He should avoid haste and the too common habit of skimming books. Reading simply gives us the material of knowledge, but it is through thinking that we make it our own. Storing the memory and training the judgment are two different things. No matter how slow and tedious the process may be, if the student at first reads slowly and understandingly, he will soon gain facility.

Some persons are omnivorous readers. As soon as they finish one book they hurry to another and so rush madly from book to book, greedily devouring their contents but not digesting them. A careful reader will read a book slowly enough to examine the writer's purpose or argument, to weigh it in his mind and to draw conclusions of his own. Such reading is worth while, and all other reading, unless merely for passing amusement, is a waste of time. In forming one's mental habits it is advisable to select only those writers who are known for clearness of style and skilful use of words. Habits are quickly and unconsciously formed from one's reading, and soon become second nature.

Every tendency to wandering of the mind should be promptly checked. The reader must keep himself alert, with his mind fastened upon the subject before him, and as often as his attention wanders he must lead it gently but firmly back again. Repeated efforts of this kind will produce the desired results. Channing says:

"Intellectual culture consists, not chiefly, as many are apt to think, in accumulating information, tho this is important, but in building up a force of thought which may be turned at will on any subjects on which we are called to pass judgment. This force is manifested in the concentration of the attention, in accurate, penetrating observation, in reducing complex subjects to their elements, in diving beneath the effect of the cause, in detecting the more subtle differences and resemblances of things, in reading the future in the present, and especially in rising from particular facts to general laws of universal truths.''

By too much reading we are likely to give over our mind to the control of others and allow them to think for us. It is better to work out our own mental sums than have them done by others. Too much reading is bewildering, and unless we think for ourselves we soon lose the power of original effort. Schopenhauer warns us that too much reading deprives the mind of its elasticity, and that ''scholars are those who have read in books; but thinkers, geniuses, enlighteners of the world and benefactors of the human race, are those who have directly read in the book of the world.''

Life is too precious and fleeting to spend it with inferior literature. Our reading should not be fitful ''like a lighted candle in a windy place,'' but be steadied and regulated by a clear persistent purpose. It may be necessary to have the counsel of others in the judicious ordering of books. If, however, we are obliged to choose for ourselves, we may critically examine the preface and table of contents of a book, to determine its value as best we can, or, like Gladstone, we may first lightly skim its contents to know whether it is what we wish or not, or we may avail ourselves of the criticisms and commendations of the book reviewers.

To make the contents of a book our very own, we should own it. Then we are at liberty to mark it as we please, to indicate special passages for easy reference, to impress important truths upon our mind, or to indicate to others the parts that have most interested us. A second careful reading of some books is necessary to a thorough grasp of their contents. A few books well read, noted, digested, and intelligently discust are worth more than a whole library of volumes indifferently read. The student must bring his attention and judgment to bear upon what he reads. He will frequently inquire of the author: Is he clear, accurate, fair-minded? Are his reasons conclusive, his inferences correct, his proofs convincing? He will observe not only the force and logic of his arguments, but the general quality of his thought, as well as his use of word, phrase, idiom, metaphor, and illustration. His attitude of mind will be critical, but he will learn all he can from his author without unduly yielding his independence of judgment.

XVIII

QUESTIONS FOR SOLUTION

The student is recommended to study the following questions and statements, and determine what answer or objection, if any, he would offer in each case.

1. Does water always run downhill?

2. Which lived first, the bird or the egg?

3. The sun will rise to-morrow, for it rose to-day.

4. Will there ever be a higher creature on earth than man?

5. Explain the difference between time and eternity.

6. Is inconceivability the criterion of impossibility?

7. Brutes are not men; therefore men are not brutes.

8. With infinities can there be degrees of comparison?

9. Every man has his price.

10. The greatest argument for immortality is God.

11. Is previous good character a presumption of innocence?

12. Nothing which is dishonorable is expedient.

13. Is there any sound made where there is no one to hear?

14. A body once set in motion will never stop unless it meet with some impediment.

15. Can a fictitious narrative establish a disputed proposition?

16. From the proposition A equals B C, do we learn the parts B C separately?

17. Is the burden of proof upon the prosecution or the defense?

18. Skill in public speaking is liable to abuse; it should not, therefore, be cultivated.

19. Does the agnostic who says, "I am,

I feel, I think,'' commit himself to belief in the unknowable?

20. Because of the numerous resemblances between the earth and other planets, is it to be inferred that the latter are inhabited because the former is?

21. We believe in God, and therefore are infinite, since the merely finite can not believe the infinite.

22. Civil authorities have no more right to command over the souls and consciences of their subjects than the master of a ship has over those of his passengers or the sailors under him.

23. As a Christian you can go to the theater if you have a very high quality of Christianity; and if you have that kind of Christianity you probably will not want to go.

24. It is not possible for a man to seek either for what he knows, or for what he knows not; inasmuch as he would not seek what he knows, at least, because he knows it, and to one in such case there

is no need of seeking; nor would he seek after what he knows not, for he knows not what he shall seek for.

25. Do the facts of Christianity betoken the presence of a higher intelligence, purpose, and might than that of man?

26. Is the life of Napoleon to be commended?

27. Are the conservative forces in our nation sufficient to insure its perpetuity?

28. Is protection or free trade the wiser policy for the United States?

29. Is a college education necessary to the highest success?

30. Was Hamlet really mad?

31. Is the theater an influence more for evil than for good?

32. What is poetry?

33. Will oratory be revived in America?

XIX

SPECIMENS OF ARGUMENTATION

A CAREFUL study of specimens of argumentation affords one of the best means of developing clearness and accuracy of thought. By observing the method by which such writers make their reasons plain the student may gradually formulate a method of his own, and learn quickly to discriminate between truth and error.

The extracts presented in the following pages will, it is believed, repay careful analysis, and at the same time suggest a larger field for investigation, in which the reader is at liberty to make his own selection. The proper procedure may be indicated thus:

1. Read the extract first in its entirety in order to secure a general idea of its contents. Look at it as you would a pic-

ture, in its unity rather than in detail. After you have read it, close the book and endeavor to recall the picture. Determine what effect it has had on your mind. Does it appear to you to be reasonable and true? Have you been sufficiently imprest to give your assent? Is your general impression clear or obscure, favorable or unfavorable? Has he interested you?

2. Read it a second time in order to judge it more particularly and in detail. Is every statement true? Is logical connection well observed? Does the writer lead you from the known to the unknown, from the certain to that which has been questioned? Does he prove each point to your satisfaction? Is there skilful use of word or phrase? Have you detected his personality in his style and argument?

3. Read the passage again to indicate such parts as you wish to commit to memory.

4. Make a list of questions bearing upon

the subject under discussion, and answer them yourself.

5. Clearly state your objections, if any, and then write out your proofs to support them.

6. Finally write a composition of your own upon the subject, and request a friend to favor you with a frank criticism of it.

The student is recommended to supplement this material with the great debate between Webster and Hayne, which may be had in several cheap editions.

I

To imagine, or rather to conceive an infinite line, is to conceive a line to whose lineal value nothing can be added, for as long as an addition to it can be conceived it is not yet infinite. Is such a line conceivable as a reality? No. Let us see why. Imagine your infinite line extending through space in opposite directions—say north and south. Now, this so-called infinite line is not infinite so long as we can conceive it increased by additional length. Let us now imagine another so-called infinite line of equal length with the first, and running parallel to it. If we add the second to the first, do we not increase its lineal value? Most certainly. Then the first line was not infinite because it admitted of addition. Nor are the two together infinite because we may imagine another parallel line and another addition and a consequent increase of lineal value. We may continue this process forever and never exhaust the possibilities—never come to a lineal value that excludes possible addition. From this you will see that you can not conceive, much less imagine, an infinite line so "readily" as you thought.—L. A. LAMBERT.

II

Once more: what are my grounds for thinking that I, in my own particular case, shall die? I am as certain of it in my own innermost mind as I am that I now live; but what is the distinct evidence on which I allow myself to be certain? how would it tell in a court of justice? how should I fare under a cross-examination upon the grounds of my certitude? Demonstration, of course, I can not have of a future event, unless by means of a divine Voice; but what logical defense can I make for that undoubting, obstinate anticipation of it, of which I could not rid myself if I tried?

First, the future can not be proved *a posteriori;* therefore, we are compelled, by the nature of the case, to put up with *a priori* argument; that is, with antecedent probability, which is by itself no logical proof. Men tell me that there is a law of death, meaning by law, a necessity; and I answer that they are throwing dust into my eyes, giving me words instead of things. What is a law but a generalized fact; and what power has the past over the future? and what power has the case of others over my own case? and how many deaths have I seen? how many ocular witnesses have imparted to me their experience of deaths, sufficient to establish what is called a law?

But let there be a law of death; so there is a law, we are told, that the planets, if let alone, would severally fall into the sun—it is the centrifugal law which hinders it, and so the centripetal law is never carried out. In like manner I am not under the law of death alone; I am under a thousand laws, if I am under one; and they thwart and counteract each other, and jointly determine the irregular line, along which my actual history runs, divergent from the special direction of any one of them. No law is carried out, except in cases where it acts freely. How do I know that the law of death will be allowed its free action in my particular case? We often are able to avert death by medical treatment: why should death have its effect, sooner or later, in every case conceivable?

It is true that the human frame, in all instances which come before me, first grows, and then declines, wastes, and decays, in visible preparation for dissolution. We see death seldom, but of this decline we are witnesses daily; still, it is a plain fact, that most men who die, die, not by any law of death, but by the law of disease; and some writers have questioned whether death is ever, strictly speaking, natural. Now, are diseases necessary? Is there any law that every one, sooner or later, must fall under the power of disease? and what would happen on a large scale were there no diseases? Is what we call the law of death anything more than the chance of disease? Is the prospect of my death, in its logical evidence—as that evidence is brought home to me—much more than a high probability?

The strongest proof I have for my inevitable mortality is the *reductio ad absurdum.* Can I point to the man, in historic times, who has lived his two hundred years? What has become of past generations of men, unless it is true that they suffered dissolution? But this is a circuitous argument to warrant a conclusion to which, in matter of fact, I adhere so relentlessly. Anyhow, there is a considerable "surplusage," as Locke calls it, of belief over proof, when I determine that I individually must die. But what logic can not do, my own personal reasoning, my good sense, which is the healthy condition of such personal reasoning, but which can not adequately express itself in words, does for me, and I am possest with the most precise, absolute, masterful certitude of my dying some day or other.

I am led on by these reflections to make another remark. If it is difficult to explain how a man knows that he shall die, is it not more difficult for him to satisfy himself how he knows he was born? His knowledge about himself does not rest on memory, nor on distinct testimony, nor on circumstantial evidence. Can he bring into one focus of proof the reasons which make him so sure? I am not speaking of scientific men, who have diverse channels of knowledge, but of an ordinary individual, as one of ourselves.

Answers doubtless may be given to some of these questions; but, on the whole, I think it is the fact that many of our most obstinate and most reasonable certitudes depend on proofs which are informal and personal, which baffle our powers of analysis, and can not be brought under logical rule, because they can not be submitted to logical statistics. If we must speak of law, this recognition of a correlation between certitude and implicit proof seems to me a law of our minds.—JOHN HENRY NEWMAN.

III

The facts with which I shall deal this evening are mainly old and familiar; nor is there anything new in the general use I shall make of them. If there shall be any novelty, it will be in the mode of presenting the facts, and the inferences and observations following that presentation. In his speech last autumn at Columbus, Ohio, as reported in the New York *Times*, Senator Douglas said:

"Our fathers, when they framed the government under which we live, understood this question just as well, and even better, than we do now."

I fully indorse this, and I adopt it as a text for this discourse. I so adopt it because it furnishes a precise and an agreed starting-point for a discussion between Republicans and that wing of the Democracy headed by Senator Douglas. It simply leaves the inquiry: What was the understanding those fathers had of the question mentioned?

What is the frame of the Government under which we live? The answer must be, "The Constitution of the United States." That Constitution consists of the original, framed in 1787, and under which the present government first went into operation, and twelve subsequent framed amendments, the first ten of which were framed in 1789.

Who were our fathers that framed the Constitution? I suppose the "thirty-nine" who signed the original instrument may be fairly called our fathers who framed that part of the present Government. It is almost exactly true to say they framed it, and it is altogether true to say they fairly represented the opinion and sentiment of the whole nation at that time. Their names, being familiar to nearly all, and accessible to quite all, need not now be repeated.

I take these "thirty-nine," for the present, as being "our fathers who framed the government under which we live." What is the question which, according to the text, those fathers understood "just as well, and even better, than we do now?"

It is this: Does the proper division of the local from Federal authority, or anything in the Constitution, forbid our Federal Government to control as to slavery in our Federal territories?

Upon this, Senator Douglas holds the affirmative, and Republicans the negative. This affirmation and denial form an issue; and this issue—this question—is precisely what the text declares our fathers understood "better than we." Let us now inquire whether the "thirty-nine," or any of them, ever acted upon this question; and if they did, how they acted upon it—how they exprest that better understanding.—ABRAHAM LINCOLN.

IV

I call on working men to take hold of the cause of temperance as peculiarly their cause. These remarks are more needed in consequence of the efforts made far and wide to annul at the present moment a recent law for the suppression of the sale of ardent spirits in such quantities as favor intemperance. I know that there are intelligent and good men who believe that, in enacting this law, Government transcends its limits, left its true path, and established a precedent for legislative interference with all our pursuits and pleasures. No one here looks more jealously on Government than myself. But I maintain that this is a case which stands by itself, which can be confounded with no other, and on which Government, from its very nature and end, is peculiarly bound to act. Let it never be forgotten then the great end of Government, its highest function, is, not to make roads, grant charters, originate improvements, but to prevent or repress crimes against individual rights and social order. For this end it ordains a penal code, erects prisons, and inflicts fearful punishments. Now, if it be true that a vast proportion of the crimes which Government is instituted to prevent and repress have their origin in the use of ardent spirits; if our poorhouses, work-houses, jails, and penitenitaries are tenanted in a great degree by those whose first and chief impulse to crime came from the distillery and dram-shop; if murder and theft, the most fearful outrages on property and life, are most frequently the issues and consummation of intemperance, is not Government bound to restrain by legislation the vending of the stimulus to these terrible social wrongs? Is Government never to act as a parent, never to remove the causes or occasions of wrong-doing? Has it but one instrument for repressing crime; namely, public, infamous punishment—an evil only inferior to crime? Is Government a usurper? Does it wander beyond its sphere, by imposing restraints on an article which does no imaginable good, which can plead no benefit conferred on body or mind, which unfits the citizen for the discharge of his duty to his country, and which, above all stirs up men to the perpetration of most of the crimes from which it is the highest and most solemn office of Government to protect society?—W. E. CHANNING.

V

Ingersoll—Logic is not satisfied with assertion.

Comment—Then it is not satisfied with your assertion in reference to it. But you are evidently ignorant of what logic means. Logic as a science deals with principles, not assertions; and logic as an art deals with assertions only. Assertions are the subject-matter on which it acts. It simply deduces conclusions from assertions or propositions called premises, and cares not whether these premises are true or false. Hence, the very reverse of what you say is true. Logic is satisfied with assertions, and knows and deals with nothing else. Your blunder arose from your confounding reason with logic. Reason deals with principles and truths, logic with assertions. That reason is not satisfied with assertions becomes more apparent the more your article on the "Christian Religion" is subjected to careful analysis.

Ingersoll—It (logic) cares nothing for the opinions of the great.

Comment—If those opinions are formulated into assertions, it does care for them, because it deals with nothing else. You meant to say: Reason cares nothing, etc. This careless use of words and confounding of terms indicates a confused and imperfect method of thinking. He who thinks with clearness and precision is not hard to understand, while a slovenly thinker leaves the reader in a state of chronic doubt as to what is meant.

Ingersoll—In the world of science a fact is a legal tender.

Comment—Then, before you can assert a legal tender, you must demonstrate a fact. A fact must be established as such before it is legal tender. Now, the question between you and the Christian is this: What are the facts? The whole controversy rests on the answer to this question. What you offer as facts, the Christian may reject as fallacies and sophistries, and what he offers as facts you may reject. It follows, therefore, that until both parties agree as to what are the facts, they can not agree as to what is legal tender. What you intended, then, as a wise saying has no practical sense in it. But for those who like that sort of thing, it is about the sort of thing they will make.

Ingersoll—A fact is a legal tender.

Comment—A counterfeit is a fact; is it legal tender? Oh! no. Well, then, a fact is not a legal tender until it is known to be a fact. What is a legal tender? It is a promise to pay which may not be worth ten cents on a dollar, but which the law compels you to accept when offered. Is this your idea of what facts are? And do you intend the facts offered by you to be received in that light? If so, perhaps you are right.

Ingersoll—Assertions and miracles are base and spurious coins.

Comment—If this be true, then the assertion you have just made is base and spurious coin. You say all assertions are base and spurious. Is it because they are assertions or because they are false? If all assertions are base and spurious, we can not believe anything whatever that is asserted, simply because it is asserted. I assert that two and two make four. This is an assertion. Is it false? Is it false? It must be, if what you say is true. From this it appears that you again failed to say what you meant; for you will certainly admit that some assertions are true—your own, for instance.

Perhaps you meant to say false assertions are base and spurious. If so, this is on a par with your legal-tender sophisms and involves the same amount of meaningless verbiage. The truth or fallacy of an assertion must be established before you can assert it to be base and spurious. But the truth or fallacy of an assertion is the question in debate. Let me illustrate: I make the assertion that the Christian religion is of divine origin. You will observe that the truth or fallacy of this assertion is the point in debate, and to assert either one or the other without proof, is to beg the question. This you do when you make the assertion that assertions are base and spurious.

But perhaps I have misunderstood you all this time. You "probably think" that all assertions favoring Christianity are base and spurious, while all those against it have the true ring. If you meant this you should have had the "courage of the soul!" to say it, and not hide your insinuation under a meaningless, commonplace phrase. I notice you are fond of making curt little maxims, which, on examination, mean nothing, unless when they cover a fallacy. They are scattered through your article so liberally as to lead one to believe you intended them for argument. But—

Ingersoll—Miracles are base and spurious coins.

Comment—That depends. And here I must make the same distinction I made in regard to assertions. If a miracle is a fact, it is not base and spurious. Now, the fact or fallacy of a miracle is the point in debate. Until that point is settled, not by assertions, but by valid arguments, you can not say that it is spurious, for when you make that assertion you simply beg the question. To beg the question in argument is like asking a knight or a castle of your opponent in a game of chess. It is a sign of conscious weakness.

Ingersoll—We have the right to rejudge the justice even of a god.

Comment—If by "a god" you mean some deity of heathen mythology, I can not stop to consider it. If you mean the infinite Being, whom Christians call God, I deny your right or competency to rejudge His justice, for reasons which I have already given, and which I need not here repeat. It is sufficient to say that the finite can not be the measure of the infinite.

Ingersoll—No one should throw away his reason—the fruit of all experience.

Comment—Your purpose here is to leave the impression that, to be a Christian, a man must throw away his reason. Man's reason is a gift of God, and God requires him to exercise and use it, and not throw it away. And he will one day ask him to give a strict account of the use he has made of it. While telling us not to throw away our reason, you give a good illustration of how it can be thrown away. Thus you say:

Ingersoll—Reason is the result of all experience.

Comment—When you make reason the result of experience you destroy its proper entity. Experience is impossible without something that experiences. What is it that experiences? Reason? No; for if reason is the result of experience, it can not exist until after the experience has been complete. What, then, is it that experiences? The individual? But the individual minus reason is incapable of apprehending experience. What, then, is it that experiences? There must be some being that experiences, for experience can not exist without a subject. The mind? But mind and reason are identical. Reason is the mind, in action. The fact is, human reason, or conscious mind, is that which experiences; it is, therefore, prior to experience, and since it is prior to experience, it can not be a result of it. Without reason experience is impossible, and, therefore, when you make reason the result of experience you throw away both reason and experience. This is the logical result of your proposition. Again you say:

Ingersoll—Reason is the fruit of all experience.

Comment—By this "all" you mean, I suppose, the experience of all mankind, together with your own. But you have barred yourself from the right to benefit by the experience of others, for that experience can be made known to you only by assertions or propositions. Now, you have declared *ex cathedra* that assertions are base and spurious coins, and rejected with contempt the statements of the dead past, by which alone the experience of the human race can be known. You have sawed off the limb on which you sit, and deprived yourself of all experience except your own.

Ingersoll—It (reason) is the intellectual capital of the soul, the only light, the only guide.

Comment—Reason is the soul or intellect itself in conscious action; hence it can not be its own intellectual capital, or its only light and guide. You seem to forget what you have said before, namely, that reason is the result of experience. Now, to say that reason is the only light and guide of the soul, and at the same time the result of experience, is to contradict yourself. What lights and guides the soul while it is experiencing? Reason? No; for you have told us that reason is the result of that experience. A result is an effect, and an effect can not be prior to its cause. It follows, then, from your own definition, that reason is not and can not be the only light or guide of the soul. But even if you had not contradicted yourself egregiously, your assertion that reason is the only light, etc., can not be accepted, for it is a pitiable begging of the whole question at issue—a denial of revelation as a guide to reason, and this you will see is the point between you and the Christian. Your statement thus cunningly assumes, as proved, that which you set out to prove. This is one of the peculiarities of your method in debate. It is on this account that I am under the necessity of analyzing almost every assertion you make.—L. A. LAMBERT.

VI

The history of thought during the present century proves that the world has come round spontaneously to the position of the first. One of the ablest philosophical schools of the day erects a whole anti-Christian system on this very doctrine. Seeking by means of it to sap the foundation of spiritual religion, it stands unconsciously as the most significant witness for its truth. What is the creed of the agnostic but the confession of the spiritual numbness of humanity? The negative doctrine which it reiterates with such sad persistency, what is it but the echo of the oldest of scientific and religious truths? And what are all these gloomy and rebellious infidelities, these touching and too sincere confessions of universal nescience, but a protest against this ancient law of death?—HENRY DRUMMOND.

XX

GOLDEN RULES IN ARGUMENTATION

1. Do not argue about everything.
2. Never belittle your opponent.
3. Control your temper.
4. Be impartial in your search for truth.
5. Seek to make a favorable impression.
6. Cultivate calmness and candor.
7. Do not resent opposition.
8. Avoid egotism.
9. Keep your eyes on all your company.
10. If you agree in part with an opponent, say so.
11. Do not be obstinate.
12. Many trifles may go unchallenged.
13. Be concise.
14. Hear others with patience, as you yourself would be heard.

15. Avoid high key.
16. Don't quibble.
17. Have a main point to prove.
18. Never fear to put the truth on trial.
19. Avoid generalization.
20. Look your hearer in the eye.
21. Do not argue with your hands.
22. Speak distinctly.
23. Avoid personalities.
24. Do not emphasize the obvious.
25. Define your terms.
26. Keep some ammunition in reserve.
27. Make a strong ending.

APPENDIX

APPENDIX

NOTE FOR A LAW LECTURE

BY ABRAHAM LINCOLN

I am not an accomplished lawyer. I find quite as much material for a lecture in those points wherein I have failed, as in those wherein I have been moderately successful. The leading rule for the lawyer, as for the man of every other calling, is diligence. Leave nothing for to-morrow which can be done to-day. Never let your correspondence fall behind. Whatever piece of business you have in hand, before stopping, do all the labor pertaining to it which can then be done. When you bring a common-law suit, if you have the facts for doing so, write the declaration at once. If a law point be involved, examine the books, and note the authority you rely on upon the declaration itself, where you are sure to find it wanted. The same of defenses and pleas. In business not likely to be litigated—ordinary collection cases, foreclosures, partitions, and the like—make all examinations of titles, and note them, and even draft orders and decrees in advance. This course has a triple advantage; it avoids omissions and neglect, saves you labor when once done, performs the labor out of court when you have leisure, rather than in court when you have not. Extemporaneous speaking should be practised and cultivated. It is the lawyer's avenue to the public. However able and faithful he may be in other respects, people are slow to bring him business if he can not make a speech. And yet there is not a more fatal error to young lawyers than relying too much on speech-making. If any one, upon his rare powers of speaking, shall claim an exemption from the drudgery of the law, his case is a failure in advance.

Discourage litigation. Persuade your

neighbors to compromise whenever you can. Point out to them how the nominal winner is often a real loser—in fees, expenses, and waste of time. As a peacemaker the lawyer has a superior opportunity of being a good man. There will be business enough.

Never stir up litigation. A worse man can scarcely be found than one who does this. Who can be more nearly a fiend than he who habitually overhauls the register of deeds in search of defects in titles, whereon to stir up strife, and put money in his pocket? A moral tone ought to be infused into the profession which should drive such men out of it.

The matter of fees is important, far beyond the mere question of bread and butter involved. Properly attended to, fuller justice is done to both lawyer and client. An exorbitant fee should never be claimed. As a general rule, never take your whole fee in advance, nor any more than a small retainer. When fully paid beforehand, you are more than a common mortal if you can feel the same interest in the case as if something was still in prospect for you, as well as for your client. And when you lack interest in the case the job will very likely lack skill and diligence in the performance. Settle the amount of fee and take a note in advance. Then you will feel that you are working for something, and you are sure to do your work faithfully and well. Never sell a fee note—at least not before the consideration service is performed. It leads to negligence and dishonesty—negligence by losing interest in the case, and dishonesty in refusing to refund when you have allowed the consideration to fail.

There is a vague popular belief that lawyers are necessarily dishonest. I say vague, because when we consider to what extent confidence and honors are reposed in and conferred upon lawyers by the people, it appears improbable that their impression of dishonesty is very distinct and vivid.

Yet the impression is common, almost universal. Let no young man choosing the law for a calling for a moment yield to the popular belief—resolve to be honest at all events; and if in your own judgment you can not be an honest lawyer, resolve to be honest without being a lawyer. Choose some other occupation, rather than one in the choosing of which you do, in advance, consent to be a knave.

OF TRUTH

By Francis Bacon

What is truth? said jesting Pilate, and would not stay for an answer. Certainly there be those that delight in giddiness, and count it a bondage to fix a belief, affecting free-will in thinking, as well as in acting. And tho the sect of philosophers of that kind be gone, yet there remain certain discoursing wits, which are of the same veins, tho there be not so much blood in them as was in those of the ancients. But it is not only the difficulty and labor which men take in finding out the truth, nor again that, when it is found, it imposeth upon men's thoughts; that doth bring lies in favor, but a natural tho corrupt love of the lie itself. One of the later school of the Grecians examineth the matter, and is at a stand to think what should be in it, that men should love lies, where neither they make for pleasure, as with poets, nor for advantage, as with the merchant; but for the lie's sake. But I can not tell; this same truth is a naked and open daylight, that doth not show the masks, and mummeries, and triumphs of the world, half so stately and daintily as candle-lights. Truth may, perhaps, come to the price of a pearl, that showeth best by day; but it will not rise to the price of a diamond or carbuncle, that showeth best in varied lights. A mixture of a lie doth ever add pleasure. Doth any man doubt that if there were taken out of men's minds vain opinions, flattering hopes, false valuations, imaginations as one would, and the like; but it would leave the minds of a number of men poor, shrunken things, full of melancholy and indisposition, and unpleasing to themselves? One of the fathers, in great severity, called poesy *vinum daemonum,* because it filleth the imagination, and yet it is but with the shadow of a lie. But it is not the lie that passeth through the mind, but the lie that sinketh in, and settleth in it, that doth the hurt, such as we spake of before. But, howsoever, these things are thus in men's depraved judgments and affections; yet truth, which only doth judge itself, teacheth that the inquiry of truth, which is the love-making, or wooing of it; the knowledge of truth, which is the presence of it, and the belief of truth, which is the enjoying of it; is the sovereign good of human nature. The first creature of God, in the works of the days, was the light of the sense; the last was the light of reason;

and his Sabbath work ever since is the illumination of His spirit. First He breathed light upon the face of the matter, or chaos; then He breathed light into the face of man, and still he breatheth and inspireth light into the face of his chosen. The poet that beautified the sect, that was otherwise inferior to the rest, saith yet excellently well: "It is a pleasure to stand upon the shore and to see ships tost upon the sea; a pleasure to stand in the window of a castle, and to see a battle, and the adventures thereof below; but no pleasure is comparable to the standing upon the vantage-ground of truth, a hill not to be commanded, and where the air is always clear and serene; and to see the errors, and wanderings, and mists, and tempests, in the vale below"; so always, that this prospect be with pity, and not with swelling or pride. Certainly, it is heaven upon earth to have a man's mind move in charity, rest in providence, and turn upon the poles of truth.

To pass from theological and philosophical truth to the truth of civil business, it will be acknowledged, even by those that practise it not, that clear and round dealing is the honor of man's nature; and that mixture of falsehood is like alloy in coin of gold and silver, which may make the metal work the better, but it embaseth it. For these winding and crooked courses are the goings of the serpent, which goeth basely upon the belly, and not upon the feet. There is no vice that doth so cover a man with shame as to be found false and perfidious. And, therefore, Montaigne saith prettily, when he inquired the reason why the word of the lie should be such a disgrace, and such an odious charge? Saith he, "If it be well weighed, to say that a man lieth is as much as to say that he is brave toward God, and a coward toward men. For a lie faces God, and shrinks from man." Surely, the wickedness of falsehood and breach of faith can not possibly be so highly exprest as in that it shall be the last peal to call the judgments of God upon the generations of men: it being foretold that when Christ cometh "He shall not find faith upon the earth."

OF PRACTISE AND HABITS

BY JOHN LOCKE

We are born with faculties and powers capable almost of anything, such at least as would carry us further than can be easily imagined; but it is only the exercise of those powers which gives us ability and skill in anything, and leads us toward perfection.

A middle-aged plowman will scarcely ever be brought to the carriage and language of a gentleman, tho his body be as well proportioned and his joints as supple, and his natural parts not any way inferior. The legs of a dancing-master, and the fingers of a musician, fall, as it were, naturally, without thought or pains, into regular and admirable motions. Bid them change their parts and they will in vain endeavor to produce like motions in the members not used to them, and it will require length of time and long practise to attain but some degree of a like ability. What incredible and astonishing actions do we find rope-dancers and tumblers bring their bodies to!—not but that sundry in almost all manual arts are as wonderful, but I name those which the world takes notice of for such, because, on that very account, they give money to see them. All these admired motions, beyond the reach, and almost the conception, of unpractised spectators, are nothing but the mere effects of use and industry in men whose bodies have nothing peculiar in them from those of the amazed lookers-on.

As it is in the body, so it is in the mind; practise makes it what it is, and most, even of those excellences which are looked on as natural endowments, will be found, when examined into more narrowly, to be the product of exercise, and to be raised to that pitch only by repeated actions. Some men are remarked for pleasantness in raillery, others for apologues and apposite diverting stories. This is apt to be taken for the effect of pure nature, and that the rather, because it is not got by rules; and those who excel in either of them never purposely set themselves to the study of it as an art to be learned. But yet it is true that at first some lucky hit which took with somebody, and gained him commendation, encouraged him to try again inclined his thoughts and endeavors that way, till at last he insensibly got a facility in it without perceiving how; and that is attributed wholly to nature, which was much more the effect of use and practise. I do not deny that natural disposition may often give the first rise to it, but that never carries a man far without use and exercise, and it is practise alone that brings the powers of the mind, as well as those of the body, to their perfection. Many a good poetic vein is buried under a trade and never produces anything for want of improvement. We see the ways of discourse and reasoning are very different, even concerning the same matter at court and in the university. And he that will go but from Westminster Hall to the Exchange will find a different genius and turn in their ways of talking; and yet one can not think that all whose lot fell in the city were born with different parts from those who were bred at the university or inns of court.

To what purpose all this, but to show that the difference so observable in men's understandings and parts does not arise so much from the natural faculties as acquired habits? He would be laughed at that should go about to make a fine dancer out of a country hedger at past fifty. And he will not have much better success who shall endeavor at that age to make a man reason well, or speak handsomely, who has never been used to it, tho you should lay before him a collection of all the best precepts of logic or oratory. Nobody is made anything by hearing of rules, or laying them up in his memory; practise must settle the habit of doing, without reflecting on the rule, and you may as well hope to make a good painter or musician extempore by a lecture and instruction in the arts of music and painting, as a coherent thinker, or strict reasoner, by a set of rules showing him wherein right reasoning consists.

This being so, that defects and weakness in men's understandings, as well as other faculties, come from a want of a right use of their own minds, I am apt to think the fault is generally mislaid upon nature, and there is often a complaint of want of parts, when the fault lies in want of a due improvement of them. We see men frequently dexterous and sharp enough in making a bargain, who, if you reason with them about matters of religion, appear perfectly stupid.

IMPROVING THE MEMORY

By Isaac Watts

Memory is a distinct faculty of the mind, very different from perception, judgment, reasoning and its other powers. Then we are said to remember anything, when the idea of it arises in the mind, with a consciousness, at the same time, that we have had this idea before. Our memory is our natural power of retaining what we learn, and of recalling it on every occasion. Therefore, we can never be said to remember anything, whether it be ideas or propositions, words or things, notions or arguments, of which we have not had some former idea or perception, either by sense or imagination, thought or reflection. Whatsoever we learn from observation, books, conversation, etc., it must be all laid up and preserved in the memory, if we would make it really useful.

So necessary and so excellent a faculty is the memory, that all other abilities of the mind borrow from it their beauty and perfection. For other capacities of the soul are almost useless without this. To what purpose are all our labors in knowledge and wisdom, if we want memory to preserve and use what we have acquired? What signify all other intellectual or spiritual improvements, if they are lost as soon as they are obtained? It is memory alone that enriches the mind, by preserving what our labor and industry daily collect. In a word, there can be neither knowledge nor arts, nor sciences, without memory; nor can there be any improvement of mankind in virtue or morals, or the practise of religion, without the assistance and influence of this power. Without memory the soul of man would be but a poor, destitute, naked being, with an everlasting blank spread over it, except the fleeting ideas of the present moment.

Memory is very useful to those who speak, as well as to those who learn. It assists the teacher and the orator, as well as the scholar or the hearer. The best speeches and instructions are almost lost, if those who hear immediately forget them. And those who are called to speak in public are much better heard and accepted when they can deliver their discourse by the help of a lively genius and a ready memory, than when they are forced to read all they would communicate. Reading is certainly a heavier way of conveying our sentiments, and there are very few mere readers who have the felicity of penetrating the soul, and awakening the passions of those who hear, by such a grace and power of oratory, as the man who seems to talk every word from his very heart, and pours out the riches of his own knowledge upon the people around him, by the help of a free and copious memory. This gives life and spirit to everything that is spoken, and has a natural tendency to make a deeper impression on the minds of men. It awakens the dullest spirits, causes them to receive a discourse with more affection and pleasure, and adds a singular grace and excellence both to the person and his oration.

A good judgment and a good memory are very different. A person may have a very strong, capacious and retentive memory, where the judgment is very weak; as sometimes it happens in those who are but one degree above an idiot, who have manifested an amazing strength and extent of memory, but have hardly been able to join or disjoin two or three ideas in a wise and happy manner to make a solid, rational proposition. There have been instances of others, who have had but a very tolerable power of memory; yet their judgment has been of much superior degree—just and wise, solid and excellent.

Yet it must be acknowledged that where a happy memory is found in any person, there is good foundation laid for a wise and just judgment of things, wherever the natural genius has anything of sagacity to make a right use of it. A good judgment must always, in some measure, depend upon a survey and comparison of several things together in the mind, and determining the truth of some doubtful proposition by that survey and comparison. When the mind has, as it were, set all those various objects present before it, which are necessary to form a true proposition or judgment concerning anything, it then determines that such and such ideas are to be joined or disjoined, to be affirmed or denied; and this in a consistency and correspondence with all those other ideas or propositions which in any way relate or belong to the same subject. Now, there can be no such comprehensive survey of many things without a tolerable degree of memory. It is by reviewing things past we learn to judge of the future. It happens, sometimes, that if one needful or important object or idea be absent, the judgment concerning the thing considered will thereby become false or mistaken.

You will inquire then, how comes it to pass, that there are some persons who appear in the world of business, as well as in the world of learning, to have a good judgment, and have acquired the just character of prudence and wisdom, and yet have neither a very bright genius, nor sagacity of thought, nor a very happy memory, so that they can not set before their mind at once a large scene of ideas, in order to pass a judgment?

Now, we may learn from Penseroso some account of this difficulty. You will scarcely ever find this man forward in judging and determining things proposed to him. He always takes time, and delays, and suspends, and ponders things maturely before he passes his judgment. Then he practises a slow meditation, ruminates on the subject, and thus, perhaps, in two or three nights and days, rouses those several ideas, one after another, as he can, which are necessary, in order to judge right of the thing proposed, and make them pass before his review in succession. This he does to relieve the want both of a quick sagacity of thought and a ready memory and speedy recollection. This cautious practise lays the foundation of his just judgment and wise conduct. He surveys well before he judges.

Whence I can not but take occasion to infer one good rule of advice to persons of higher as well as lower genius, and of large as well as narrow memories, namely, that they do not too hastily pronounce concerning matters of doubt or inquiry, where there is not an urgent necessity of present action. The bright genius is ready to be so forward, as often betrays itself into great errors in judgment, speech, and conduct, without a continual guard upon itself, and using the bridle of the tongue. And it is by this delay and precaution that many a person of much lower natural abilities will often excel persons of the brightest genius in wisdom and prudence.

It is often found that a fine genius has but feeble memory. For where the genius is bright, and the imagination vivid, the power of memory may be too much neglected and lose its improvement. An active fancy readily wanders over a multitude of objects, and is continually entertaining itself with new flying images. It runs through a number of new scenes or new pages with pleasure, not without due attention, and seldom suffers itself to dwell long enough upon any one of them to make a deep impression upon the mind, and commit it to lasting remembrance, This is one plain and obvious reason why there are some persons of very bright parts and active spirits, who have but short and narrow powers of remembrance; for, having riches of their own, they are not solicitous to borrow.

As such a quick and various fancy and invention may be some hindrance to the attention and memory, so a mind of a good retentive ability, and which is ever crowding its memory with things which it learns and reads continually, may prevent, restrain, and cramp the invention itself. The memory of Lectorides is ever ready, upon all occasions, to offer to his mind something out of other men's writings or conversations, and is presenting him with the thoughts of other persons perpetually. Thus the man who has naturally a good flowing invention does not suffer himself to pursue his own thoughts. Some persons who have been blest by nature with sagacity and no contemptible genius, have too often forbid the exercise of it, by tying themselves down to the memory of the volumes they have read, and the sentiments of other men contained in them. Where the memory has been almost constantly employing itself gathering new acquirements, and where there has not been a judgment sufficient to distinguish what things were fit to be recommended and treasured up in the memory, and what things were idle, useless, or needless, the mind has been filled with a wretched heap and mixture of words or ideas; and the soul may be said to have had large possessions, but no true riches.

I have read in some of Mr. Milton's writings a very beautiful simile, whereby he represents the books of the fathers, as they are called in the Christian Church. "Whatsoever," says he, "Old Time, with his huge drag-net, has conveyed down to us along the stream of ages, whether it be shells or shellfish, jewels or pebbles, sticks or straws, seaweeds or mud, these are the ancients, these are the fathers." The case is much the same with the memorial possessions of the greatest part of mankind. A few useful things, perhaps, mixed and confounded with many trifles and all manner of rubbish, fill up their memories and compose their intellectual possessions. It is a great happiness, therefore, to distinguish things aright, and to lay up nothing in the memory but what has some just value in it, and is worthy to be numbered as a part of our treasure.

Whatever improvements are to the mind of man from the wise exercise of his own reasoning powers, these may be called his proper manufactures; and whatever he borrows from abroad, these may be termed his foreign treasures. Both together make a wealthy and happy mind.

How many excellent judgments and reasonings are framed in the mind of a man of wisdom and study in a length of years! How many worthy and admirable notions has he been possest of in life, both by his own reasonings and by his prudent and laborious collections in the course of his reading! But alas! how many thousands of them vanish away, and are lost for want of a more retentive memory! When a young practitioner in the law was once said to contest a point in debate with that great lawyer in the last age, Seargeant Maynard, he is reported to have answered him, "Alas! young man, I have forgot much more law than ever thou hast learned or read."

What an unknown and unspeakable happiness would it be to a man of judgment, and who is engaged in the pursuit of knowledge, if he had but a power of stamping all his own best sentiments upon his memory in some indelible characters, and if he could not imprint every valuable paragraph and sentiment of the most excellent authors he has read, upon his mind, with the same speed and facility with which he read them! If a man of good genius and sagacity could not retain and survey all those numerous, those wise and beautiful ideas at once, which have ever passed through his mind upon one subject, how admirably would he be furnished to pass a just judgment about all present objects and occurrences! What a glorious entertainment and pleasure would fill and felicitate his spirit if he could grasp all these in a single survey, as the skilful eye of a painter runs over a fine and complicate piece of history, wrought by the hand of a Titian or a Raffael, views the whole scene at once and feeds himself with the extensive delight! But these are joys which do not belong to mortality.

Thus far I have indulged some loose and unconnected thoughts and remarks with regard to the different powers of wit, memory and judgment, for it was very difficult to throw them into a regular form or method without more room. Let us now, with more regularity, treat of the memory alone.

Tho the memory is a natural faculty of the mind of man and belongs to spirits which are not incarnate, yet it is greatly assisted or hindered, and much diversified by the brain or the animal nature, to which the soul is united in this present state. But what part of the brain that is, wherein the images of things lie treasured up, is very hard for us to determine with certainty. It is most probable that those very fibers, pores, or traces of the brain, which assist at the first idea or perception of any object, are the same which assist also at the recollection of it; and then it will follow that the memory has no special part of the brain devoted to its own service, but uses all those parts in general which subserve our sensations, as well as our thinking and reasoning powers.

As the memory improves in young persons from their childhood, and decays in old age, so it may be increased by art and labor, and proper exercise; or it may be injured and quite spoiled by sloth, or by disease, or a stroke on the head. There are some reasonings on this subject which make it evident that the goodness of a memory depends, in a great degree, upon the consistence and the temperament of that part of the brain which is appointed to assist the exercise of all our sensible and intellectual faculties. So, for instance, in children: they perceive and forget a hundred things in an hour. The brain is so soft that it receives immediately all impressions, like water or liquid mud, and retains scarcely any of them. All the traces, forms, or images, which are drawn there, are immediately effaced or closed up again, as tho you wrote with your finger on the surface of a river or on a vessel of oil.

On the contrary, in old age men have a very feeble remembrance of things that were done of late, that is, the same day, or week, or year. The brain is grown so hard that the present images or strokes make little or no impression, and therefore immediately vanish. Prisco, in his seventy-eighth year, will tell long stories of things done when he was in the battle of the Boyne, almost fifty years ago, and when he studied at Oxford, seven years before. For those impressions were made when the brain was more susceptive. They have been deeply engraven at the proper season, and therefore they remain. But words or things which he lately spoke or did are immediately forgotten because the brain is now grown more dry and solid in its consistence, and receives not much more impression than if you wrote with your finger on a floor of clay, or a plastered wall.

But in the middle stage of life, or it may be from fifteen to fifty years of age, the memory is generally in its happiest state; the brain easily receives and long retains the images and traces which are imprest upon it, and the natural spirits are more active to range these little infinite unknown figures of things in their proper cells or cavities, to preserve and recollect them.

Whatever, therefore, keeps the brain in its best consistence may be a help to preserve the memory. But excess of wine, or luxury of any kind, as well as excess in study or business, may overwhelm the memory by overstraining and weakening the fibers of the brain, wasting the spirits, injuring the consistence of that tender substance, and confounding the images that are laid up there.

A good memory has these several qualifications: 1. It is ready to admit, with great ease, the various ideas, both of words and things, which are learned or taught. 2. It is large and copious to treasure up these ideas in great number and variety. 3. It is strong and durable, to retain for a considerable time those words or thoughts which are committed to it. 4. It is faithful and active to suggest and recollect, upon every proper occasion, all those words or thoughts which have been recommended to its care, or treasured up in it.

Now, in every one of these qualifications a memory may be injured or improved. Yet I shall not insist distinctly on these particulars, but only in general propose a few rules or directions, whereby this noble faculty may be preserved or assisted, and show what are the practises that, both by reason and experience, have been found of happy influence to this purpose.

There is one great and general direction, which belongs to the improvement of other powers, as well as of the memory; and that is, to keep it always in due and proper exercise. Many acts by degrees form a habit, and thereby the ability or power is strengthened and made more ready to be again in action. Our memories should be used and inured from childhood to bear a moderate quantity of knowledge, let into them early, and they will thereby become strong for use and service. As any limb, duly exercised, grows stronger, the nerves of the body are corroborated thereby. Milo took up a calf and daily carried it on his shoulders. As the calf grew his strength grew also, and he at last arrived at firmness enough to bear the ox.

Our memories will be, in a great measure, molded and formed, improved or injured, according to the exercise of them. If we never use them they will be almost lost. Those who are wont to converse or read about a few things only, will retain but a few in their memory. Those who are used to remember things but for an hour and charge their memories with it no longer, will retain them but an hour. Let words be remembered as well as things, that so you may acquire a copiousness of language, as well as of thought, and be more ready to express your mind on all occasions.

Yet there should be a caution given in some cases. The memory of a child, or any infirm person, should not be overburdened; for a joint or a limb may be overstrained by being too much loaded, and its natural power never be recovered. Teachers should wisely judge of the power and constitution of youth, and impose no more on them than they are able to bear with cheerfulness and improvement.

And particularly they should take care that the memory of the learner be not too much crowded with a tumultuous heap or overbearing multitude of documents or ideas at one time. This is the way to remember nothing. One idea effaces another. An over-greedy grasp does not retain the largest handful. But it is the exercise of memory with a due moderation that is one general method toward its improvement.

The particular rules are such as these:

1. Due attention and diligence to understand things which we would commit to memory, is a rule of great necessity in this case. When the attention is strongly fixt to any particular subject, all that is

said concerning it makes a deeper impression upon the mind. There are some persons who complain they can not remember divine or human discourses which they hear, when, in truth, their thoughts are wandering half the time; or they hear with such coldness and indifference, and a trifling temper of spirit, that it is no wonder the things which are read, or spoken, make but a slight impression on the brain and get no firm footing in the memory, but soon vanish and are lost.

It is needful, therefore, if we would maintain a long remembrance of the things which we read or hear, that we should engage our delight in those subjects, and use the methods which are already prescribed, in order to fix the attention. Sloth and idleness will no more bless the mind with intellectual riches than it will fill the hand with grain, the field with corn, or the purse with treasure.

Let it be added, also, that not only the slothful and the negligent deprive themselves of proper knowledge for the furniture of their memory, but such as appear to have active spirits, who are ever skimming over the surface of things with a volatile temper, will fix nothing in their mind. Vario will spend whole mornings in running over loose and unconnected pages, and with fresh curiosity is ever glancing over new words and ideas that strike his present fancy. He is fluttering over a thousand objects of art and science, and yet treasures up but little knowledge. There must be the labor and the diligence of close attention to particular subjects of thought and inquiry, which only can impress what we read or think of upon the remembering faculty in man.

2. Clear and distinct apprehension of the things which we commit to memory is necessary in order to make them dwell there. If we would remember words, or learn the names of persons or things, we should have them recommended to our memory by clear and distinct pronuncia-

tion, spelling, or writing. If we would treasure up the ideas of things, notions, propositions, arguments, and sciences, these should be recommended also to our memory by a clear and distinct perception of them. Faint, glimmering and confused ideas will vanish like images seen in twilight. Everything which we learn should be conveyed to the mind in the plainest expressions, without any ambiguity, that we may not mistake what we desire to remember. This is a general rule, whether we would employ the memory about words or things; tho it must be confest that mere sounds and words are much harder to fix in the mind than the knowledge of things.

For this reason take heed, as I have often before warned you, that you do not take up with words, instead of things, nor mere sounds, instead of sentiments and ideas. Many a lad forgets what has been taught him merely because he never well understood it. He never clearly and distinctly took in the meaning of those sounds and syllables which he was required to get by heart.

This is one reason why boys make so poor a proficiency in learning the Latin tongue under masters who teach them by grammars and rules written in Latin. And this is a common case with children when they learn their catechisms in their early days. The language and the sentiments conveyed in those catechisms are far above the understandings of creatures of that age; and they have no clear ideas from the words. This makes the answers much harder to be remembered, and in truth they learn nothing but words, without ideas; and if they are ever so perfect in repeating the words, yet they know nothing of divinity.

For this reason it is necessary, in teaching children the principles of religion, that they should be exprest in very plain, easy and familiar words, brought as low as possible down to their understandings, according to their different ages and capacities, and thereby they will obtain some useful knowledge when the words are treasured up in their memory, because, at the same time, they will treasure up those divine ideas too.

3. Method in the things we commit to memory is necessary, in order to make them take more effectual possession of the mind, and abide there long. As much as systematical learning is decried by some vain and humorous triflers of the age, it is certainly the happiest way to furnish the mind with a variety of knowledge.

Whatever you would trust to your memory, let it be disposed in a proper method, connected well together, and referred to distinct and particular heads or classes, both general and particular. An apothecary's boy will much sooner learn all the medicines in his master's shop, when they are ranged in boxes or on shelves, according to their distinct natures, whether herbs, drugs, or minerals, whether leaves or roots, whether chemical or galenical preparations, whether simple or compound, etc., and when they are placed in some order, according to their nature, their fluidity, or their consistence, etc., in vials, bottles, gallipots, cases, drawers, etc. So the genealogy of a family is more easily learned when you begin at some great grandfather as the root, and distinguish the stock, the large boughs, the lesser branches, the twigs, and the buds, till you come down to the present infants of the house. And, indeed, all sorts of arts and sciences, taught in a method are more easily committed to the mind or memory.

I might give another plain simile to confirm the truth of this. What horse or carriage can take up and bear away all the various, rude and unwieldy loppings of a branchy tree at once? but if they are divided yet further, so as to be laid close and bound up in a more uniform manner into several fagots, perhaps those loppings may be all carried as one single load or burden.

The mutual dependence of things on each other helps the memory of both. A wise connection in the parts of a discourse and a rational method, give great advantage to the reader or hearer, in that they help his remembrance of it. Therefore, many mathematical demonstrations in a long train may be remembered much better than a heap of sentences which have no connection. The Book of Proverbs, at least from the tenth chapter and onward, is much harder to remember than the Book of Psalms, for this reason; and some Christians have told me that they remember what is written in the Epistle to the Romans, and that to the Hebrews, much better than many others of the sacred epistles, because there is more exact method and connection observed in them.

He that would learn to remember a

sermon which he hears, should acquaint himself by degrees with the method in which the several important parts of it are delivered. It is a certain fault, in a multitude of preachers, that they utterly neglect method; or, at least, they refuse to render their method visible and sensible to the hearers. One would be tempted to think it was for fear their auditors should remember too much of their sermons, and prevent their preaching them three or four times over. But I have candor enough to persuade myself that the true reason is, they imagine it to be a more modish way of preaching without particulars. I am sure it is a much more useless one. And it would be of great advantage, both to the speaker and hearer, to have discourses for the pulpit cast into a plain and easy method, and the reasons or inferences ranged in proper order, and that under the words *first, secondly and thirdly,* however they may be now fancied to sound unpolite or unfashionable. But

Archbishop Tillotson did not think so in his days.

A frequent review and careful repetition of the things we would learn, and an abridgment of them in a narrow compass, has a great influence to fix them in the memory. Therefore it is that the rules of grammar and useful examples of the variations of words, and the peculiar forms of speech in any language, are so often appointed by the masters, as lessons for the scholars, to be repeated; and they are contracted into tables for frequent review, that what is not fixt in the mind at first may be stamped upon the memory by the employment of a perpetual survey and rehearsal.

Repetition is so very useful a practise that Mnemon, even from his youth to his old age, never read a book without making some small points, dashes, or hooks, in the margin, to mark what parts of the discourse were proper for a review, and when he came to the end of a section or chapter, he always shut his book and recollected all the sentiments or expressions he had marked, so that he could give a tolerable analysis and abstract of every treatise he had read, just after he had finished it. Thence he became so well furnished with a rich variety of knowledge.

Even when a person is hearing a sermon or a lecture, he may give his thoughts leave now and then to step back so far as to recollect the several heads of it from the beginning, two or three times, before it is finished. The omission or loss of a sentence or two among the amplifications is richly compensated by preserving in the mind the method and order of the whole discourse, in the most important branches of it.

If we would fix in the memory the discourses we hear, or what we design to speak, let us abstract them into brief compends, and review them often. Lawyers and divines have need of such assistances.

They write down short notes or hints of the principal heads of what they desire to commit to memory, in order to preach or plead. For such abstracts and epitomes may be reviewed much sooner, and the several amplifying sentiments or sentences will be more easily invented or recollected in their proper places. The art of *short-hand* is of excellent use for this, as well as other purposes. It must be acknowledged that those who scarcely ever take a pen in their hands to write short notes or hints of what they are to speak or learn; who never try to cast things into method, or to contract the survey of them, in order to commit them to memory, need a double degree of power to retain and to recollect what they read, or hear, or even intend to speak.

Do not plunge yourself into other businesses or studies, amusements or recreations, immediately after you have attended upon instruction, if you can avoid it. Get time, if possible, to recollect the things you have heard, that they may not be washed all away from the mind by a torrent of other occurrences or engagements, nor lost in the crowd or clamor of other loud and important affairs.

Talking over the things which you have read, with your companions, on the first proper opportunity, is a most useful manner of review or repetition, in order to fix them upon the mind. Teach them to your younger friends, in order to establish your own knowledge, while you communicate it to them. The animal powers of your tongue and of your ear, as well as your intellectual faculties, will all join to help the memory. Hermetas studied hard in a remote corner of the land, and in solitude; yet he became a very learned man. He seldom was so happy as to enjoy suitable society at home, and therefore he talked over to the fields and the woods in the evening what he had been reading in the day, and found so considerable advantage by this practise, that he recommended it to all his friends since he could set his approbation to it from seventeen years' trial.

Delight in the things we learn gives great assistance toward the remembrance of them. Whatever, therefore, we desire a child should commit to memory, make it as pleasant to him as possible; endeavor to search his genius and his temper, and let him take in the instruction you give him, or the lessons you appoint him, as far as may be, in a way suited to his natural inclinations. Fabellus would never learn any moral lesson, till they were molded into the form of some fable, like those of Æsop, or till they put on the appearance of a parable, like those wherein our blest Savior taught the ignorant. Then he remembered well the emblematical instructions that were given him, and learned to practise the moral sense and meaning. Young Spectorius was taught virtue by setting before him a variety of examples of the various good qualities in human life, and he was appointed daily to repeat some story of this kind out of Valerius Maximus. The same lad was early instructed to avoid the common vices and follies of youth in the same manner. This is akin to the method whereby the Lacedemonians trained up their children to hate drunkenness and intemperance, namely, by bringing a drunken man into their company and showing them what a beast he had made of himself. Such visible and sensible forms of instruction will make long and useful impressions upon the memory.

Children may be taught to remember many things in a way of sport and play. Some young creatures have learned their letters and syllables, and the pronouncing and spelling of words, by having them pasted or written upon many little flat tablets or dies. Some have been taught vocabularies of different languages, having a word in one tongue written on one side of these tablets and the same word in another tongue written on the other side of them. There might be also many entertaining contrivances for the instruction of children in several things relating to geometry, geography and astronomy. By the employment of such alluring methods, a most agreeable and lasting impression would be made on their minds.

6. The memory of useful things may receive considerable aid if they are thrown into verse. For the numbers, and measures, and rime, according to the poesy of different languages, have a considerable influence upon mankind, both to make them receive with more ease the things proposed to their observation and preserve them longer in their remembrance. How many are there of the common affairs of life which have been taught in early years by the help of rime, and have been, like nails, fastened in a sure place, and riveted by daily use?

So the number of the days of each month is engraven on the memory of thousands and thousands of people by these four lines:

> Thirty days hath September,
> April, June, and November;
> February twenty-eight alone;
> And all the rest have thirty-one.

So have rules of health been prescribed in the book called "Schola Salernitana"; and many a person has preserved himself doubtless from evening gluttony, and the pains and diseases consequent upon it, by these four lines:

> To be easy all night,
> Let your supper be light;
> Or else you'll complain
> Of a stomach in pain.

And a hundred proverbial sentences, in various languages, are formed into rime or verse, whereby they are made to remain in the memory of old and young.

It is from this principle that moral rules have been cast into a poetic mold from all antiquity. So the golden verses of the Pythagoreans, in Greek; Cato's distiches *De Moribus,* in Latin; Lilly's precepts to scholars, called *Qui mihi,* with many others; and this has been with very good success. A line or two of this kind, recurring to the memory, has often guarded youth from a temptation to vice and folly, as well as put them in mind of their present duty.

7. When you would remember new things or words, endeavor to associate them with some words or things which you have well known before, and which are established in your memory. This association of ideas is of great importance, and may be of excellent use in many instances of human life. One idea which is familiar to the mind, connected with others which are new and strange, will bring those new ideas into easy remembrance. Maronides had got the first hundred lines of Virgil's Æneid printed upon his memory so perfectly that he

knew not only the order and number of every verse from one to a hundred, but the order and number of every word in each verse also; and by this means he would remember two or three hundred names of persons or things by some rational or fantastic connection between some word in the verse, and some letter, syllable, property, or accident of the name or thing to be remembered even tho they had been repeated but once or twice in his hearing. Animato practised much the same art of memory, by getting the Latin names of twenty-two animals into his head, according to the alphabet, namely, asinus, basilicus, canis, draco, elephas, felis, gryphus, hircus, juvencus, leo, mulus, noctua, ovis, panthera, quadrupes, rhinoceros, simia, taurus, ursus, xiphias, hyena or yena, zibetta. Most of these he divided also into four parts, namely, head and body, feet and fins, or wings, and tail; and by some arbitrary or chimerical attachment of each of these to a word or thing which he desired to remember, he committed them to the care of his memory, and that with good success.

It is also by this association of ideas that we may better imprint any new idea upon the memory, by joining with it some circumstance of the time, place, company, etc., wherein we first observed, heard, or learned it. If we would recover an absent idea, it is useful to recollect those circumstances of time, place, etc. The substance will many times be recovered and brought to the thoughts by recollecting the shadow. A man recurs to our fancy by remembering his garment, his size or stature, his office or employment, etc.; a beast, bird, or fish, by its color, figure, or motion, by the cage, or court-yard, or cistern, wherein it was kept.

To this head, also, we may refer that remembrance of names and things which may be derived from our recollection of their likeness to other things which we know; either their resemblance in the name, character, form, accident, or anything that belongs to them. An idea or word which has been lost or forgotten has been often recovered by hitting upon some kindred word or idea, which has the nearest resemblance to it, and that in the letters, syllables, or sound of the name as well as properties of the thing.

If we would remember Hippocrates, or Galen, or Paracelsus, think of a physician's name beginning with H, G or P. If we would remember Ovidius Naso, we may represent a man with a great nose; if Plato, we may think upon a person with large shoulders; if Crispus, we may fancy another with curled hair, and so of other things.

And sometimes a new or strange idea may be fixt in the memory by considering its contrary or opposite. So if we cannot hit on the word Goliath, the remembrance of David may recover it; or the name of a Trojan may be recovered by thinking of a Greek, etc.

8. In such cases, wherein it may be done, seek after a local memory or a remembrance of what you have read by the side or page where it is written or printed, whether the right or the left, whether at the top, the middle, or the bottom; whether at the beginning of a chapter or a paragraph, or at the end of it. It has been some advantage for this reason to accustom ourselves to books of the same edition, and it has been of constant and special use to divines and private Christians, to be furnished with several Bibles of the same edition; that wherever they are, whether in their chamber, parlor, or study, in the younger or elder years of life, they may find the chapters and verses in the same parts of the page.

This is also a great convenience to be observed by printers in the new editions of grammars, psalms, Testaments, etc., to print every chapter, paragraph or verse in the same part of the page as the former that so it may yield a happy assistance to those young learners who find, and even feel, the advantage of a local memory.

9. Let everything we desire to remember be fairly and distinctly written and divided into periods, with large characters; for by this means we shall the more readily imprint the matter and words on our minds and recollect them with a glance, the more remarkable the writing appears to the eye. This sense conveys the ideas to the fancy better than any other, and what we have seen is not so soon forgotten as what we have only heard.

For the assistance of weak memories, the first letters or words of every period, in every page, may be written in distinct colors, yellow, green, red, black, etc., and if you observe the same order of colors in the following sentences it may be still the better. This will make a greater impression and may much aid the memory.

APPENDIX

Under this head we may take notice of the advantage which the memory gains by having the several objects of our learning drawn out into schemes and tables. Matters of mathematical science and natural philosophy are not only let into the understanding, but preserved in the memory by figures and diagrams. The situation of the several parts of the earth are better learned by one day's conversing with a map or sea chart, than by merely reading the description of their situation a hundred times over in books of geography. So the constellations in astronomy and their position in the heavens, are more easily remembered by hemispheres of the stars well drawn. It is by having such memorials, figures and tablets hung round our studies or places of resort, that our memory of these things will be greatly assisted and improved, as I have shown at large in the twentieth chapter of the "Use of the Sciences."

I might add here, also, that once writing

over what we design to remember, and giving due attention to what we write, will fix it more in the mind than reading it five times. And in the same manner, if we had a plan of the naked lines of longitude and latitude, projected on the meridian printed for this use, a learner might much more speedily advance himself in the knowledge of geography by his own drawing the figures of all the parts of the world upon it by imitation, than by many days' survey of a map of the world so printed. The same also may be said concerning the constellations of the heavens, drawn by the learner on a naked projection of the circles of the spheres upon the plane of the equator.

10. It has sometimes been the practise of men to imprint names or sentences on their memory by taking the first letter of every word of that sentence or of those names and making a new word out of them. So the name *Maccabees* is borrowed from the first letters of the Hebrew

words which make that sentence *Mi Camoka Bealim Jehovah,* that is, *Who is like thee among the gods, O Jehovah?* which was written on their banners. So the word *vibgyor* teaches us to remember the order of the seven original colors as they appear by the sunbeams, cast through a prism on a white paper, or formed by the sun in a rainbow, according to the different refrangibility of the rays, namely, violet, indigo, blue, green, yellow, orange, red.

Other artificial helps to the memory may be just mentioned here.

Dr. Grey, in his book called "Memoria Technica," has exchanged the figures 1, 2, 3, 4, 5, 6, 7, 8, 9, for some consonants, *b, d, t, f, l, y, p, k, n,* and some vowels, *a, e, i, o, u,* and several diphthongs, and thereby formed words that denote numbers which may be easily remembered. Mr. Lowe has improved his scheme in a small pamphlet called "Mnemonics Delineated," whereby, in seven leaves, he has comprized almost an infinity of things in science and in common life, and reduced them to a sort of measure, like Latin Verse, tho the words may be supposed to be very barbarous, being such a mixture of vowels and consonants as are very unfit for harmony.

But, after all, the very writers on this subject have confest that several of these artificial helps of memory are so cumbersome as not to be suitable to every temper or person; nor are they of any use for the delivery of a discourse by memory, nor of much service in learning the sciences, but they may be sometimes practised for assisting our remembrance of certain sentences, numbers or names.

THE END.